THE TALE OF
TWO SUPPLY CHAINS

Leveraging Supplier value using
Toyota's Ecosystem approach and
GM's Cost Margin game plan

A business novel by Dr. Shawn Paul

© Shawn Paul, 2019 and 2020.

All rights reserved.

All rights reserved by the author. No part of this publication may be reproduced, stored in a retreval system or transmitted in any form or by any means, electronic, mechanical, photocopying, recording or otherwise, without the prior permission of the author.

Although every precaution has been taken to verify the accuracy of the information contained herein, the author and the publisher assume no responsibility for any errors or omissions. No liability is assume for damages that may result from the use of the information contained within.

First published in India, September 2019.
First published in the US, Nov 2020.

Blue ribbon publishers, India.

Supply Chain Revolution Press, USA.

Cover Design:
Jonathan JP Paul

Cover Credits:
www.gograph.com/gg101519760

-The tale of two supply chains: Toyota and GM-

Dedication

This book is dedicated to Neil Armstrong (1930-2012),
who was my teacher and mentor,
while at Purdue University.
He was known for his courage,
adventure sprit and perseverance.
His positivity and uncanny common sense
were contagious.

-The tale of two supply chains: Toyota and GM-

-The tale of two supply chains: Toyota and GM-

Table of Contents

Dedication 3

Table of Contents 5

Acknowledgment 9

PART 1: THE SUPPLY CHAIN - TOYOTA AND GM 11

   Prelude 13

   Disclaimer 19

   Premise 21

   Cast of Characters 23

   Chapter 1: Kevin's visit to the plant 25

   Chapter 2: Kevin's findings 39

   Chapter 3: Kevin and supply chain problem solving 47

   Chapter 4: Steve's Dilemma 57

   Chapter 5: Steve's plan 67

   Chapter 6: Kevin and Steve meet Neil 77

   Chapter 7: Balancing logistics with JIT 87

   Chapter 8: When lean meets constraints 97

   Chapter 9: A Small supplier's guide to survival 105

   Chapter 10: Minimizing variation 111

   Chapter 11: Steve deals with Supplier capacity 121

   Chapter 12: Tesla versus Everybody 131

   Chapter 13: Supply Chain Round Table 139

CHAPTER 14: KEVIN AND STEVE GO TO GLIDER TRAINING 147

CHAPTER 15: DEATH OF A LEGEND...153

CHAPTER 16: INTRODUCING JISHUKEN PROBLEM SOLVING..........157

CHAPTER 17: CREATING PERFORMANCE METRICS 165

CHAPTER 18: KEVIN & STEVE AT THE PHI DELT DINNER.............173

PART 2: AUTHOR'S NOTES 177

CHAPTER 19: AN INTERVIEW WITH THE AUTHOR...........................179

Interviewer> First of all, why is this book presented as a study of contrasts? 179

Interviewer> In your view, what are the key differences between Toyota's Supply Chain philosophy and General Motors? 179

Interviewer> How can the lessons learned in the Automotive Supply Chain help any business Supply Chain?..180

Interviewer> You are recommending a better supplier relationship. How do you go about creating a better relationship? 181

Interviewer> What are the results that you have seen with such a supplier relationship improvement?..182

Interviewer> Before we get into Collective mutualism, let me ask, is there a hierarchy of value that a supplier brings to a relationship? 183

Interviewer> How do you evaluate supplier maturity? 186

Interviewer> How is the hierarchy of supplier relationships different between Asia and the US? 188

Interviewer> Contrast the Ecosystem model to Cost benefit model? 190

Interviewer> How do you unlock the benefits of a better relationship?..192

Interviewer> How do you optimize the supplier relationship using synergy index? 195

Interviewer> Give me some examples of the Jishuken network? .196

Interviewer> What is the background research for this book?......196

Interviewer> What is the Theory of Collective Mutualism?............198

Interviewer> In your doctorate thesis, you have compared the Theory of Collective Mutualism to the evolution theory of Endosymbiosis? How does it compare?...198

Interviewer> Granted that you have a good sample of supplier accounts. Can you get the account right with just the supplier accounts? 199

APPENDIX 201

GLOSSARY & ABBREVIATIONS 203

RECOMMENDED READING 207

REFERENCES 209

-The tale of two supply chains: Toyota and GM-

Acknowledgment

Over the course of my career, I have been fortunate to be surrounded with several astute teachers and mentors. Chief among those was Neil Armstrong, Astronaut, Engineer, Pilot, Teacher, and the first man on the moon. Known for his steely nerves and deep insights, his simple suggestions helped me immensely in work and in life, while I was at Purdue.

Neil was a Purdue Alum and a frequent visitor to the campus. He was there at many home games, especially when Purdue played Ohio State. He was an inspiration and a cheerleader for the University Marching band, with the world's "largest drum".

I thank my parents and my family for their support during the writing of this book. My wife, Sarah, and my kids, Crystal and Jonathan, were very encouraging and supportive during my expat assignments to Asia and late nights that I was up at my computer, while writing this book.

-Shawn Paul
Email: BusinessSmartSupplyChain@gmail.com

-The tale of two supply chains: Toyota and GM-

Supply Chain Management

Part 1

The Supply Chain Story: Toyota and GM

-The tale of two supply chains: Toyota and GM-

Supply Chain Management

-The tale of two supply chains: Toyota and GM-

Prelude

This is a book about business competition. Companies gain an edge by investing in key strategic resources. Each such strategic investment is intended to create a competitive weapon for the Company. At the end of the day, the resource investment strategy that brings the greatest bang will raise the company to the next level. This book investigates a so-far hidden competitive weapon, especially in the resource intensive Automotive industry. We will also explore how non-automotive industries can benefit from this process.

Since the late 1990s, Toyota has been recognized for its product quality. JD Power initial quality surveys and the Consumer report's best buy recommendations clearly demonstrate Toyota's quality leadership position. Toyota's product and business competitive tools have been widely researched and even superseded by others. Lean or Toyota Production System and Six sigma have evolved as the leading drivers in problem solving and operational excellence.

New product technology and design advantages have been led by a hierarchy of suppliers, who share the same with other automakers. Such sharing helps the suppliers to reduce product cost by spreading the initial investment over a higher volume production. So, the strategic significance of these new product initiatives in Toyota's competitive plan is limited. The weapon that has been the most difficult to copy has been the Supply Chain advantage.

While Toyota's Supply Chain is unique in its structure, General Motors has also developed its own unique Supply Chain targeting its goals. We will review both Supply Chains in detail in this book.

"The ultimate competitive weapon is

... Not product development: New technologies evolve together,

... Not production: Vehicle plants follows same methodologies,

... Not sales distribution: Dealers are independent & self-driven,

... but is the Supply Chain." Prof. Wilfred D Paul, Annamalai University (about the Auto industry).

So how is Supply Chain different. First, let's take the industry metrics. On the front end, it should be clear that the working relationship between the Automakers and the suppliers is substantially different between Toyota and General Motors. Plant Moran, (previously John Henke of Planning Perspectives), publishes an annual rating for supplier relationship, called the Working Relationship Index (WRI). The interesting aspect of this index is that it covers more than 1000 buying situations, that rank each Automaker on 17 unique criteria. They range from an open and honest supplier communication to the supplier being able to recover from cancelled or delayed engineering programs.
Toyota and Honda have topped the study every year since its inception in 2002. The unfortunate situation is that 85% of the suppliers rate GM, Ford and Fiat Chrysler Automakers as "poor".

Several studies including McKinsey (OESA/McKinsey study, 2003) have estimated the direct loss of 5 to 10% of the program cost and 80% of the program waste is due to interface issues, in day to day activities between the Automaker and the supplier. This is estimated at several billion dollars per year across the industry. So, the key learning should be that the supplier

-The tale of two supply chains: Toyota and GM-

relationship and management can add so much more value to the product innovation, quick execution, product quality and successful launch of new products.

Company	2002	2020	2021	% lag
Toyota	296	345	347	Best
GM	251	269	289	16.7%
FCA	248	198	170	50.1%

Table of WRI Index for automakers,
from 2002 as the starting point.

On the other hand, General Motors, Ford and FCA have focused on establishing a higher relative priority on cost margins. Under this game plan, suppliers are awarded the business based on an acceptable quality, and superior pricing. This offers a different philosophy in competitiveness. As we will see throughout this book, these starting philosophies yields a whole different set of strategies for these companies, with the resulting product strengths being substantially different.

> *"Every breakthrough business idea begins with solving a common problem. The bigger the problem, the bigger the opportunity."* - Michael Dell (On the scope of supply chain).

The intent of this book is to explore each of these Supply Chain strategies and identify competitive advantages for your organization. While the initial premise focuses on Automotive

-The tale of two supply chains: Toyota and GM-

companies, these strategies work well for any company, automotive or otherwise.

This book is presented as a book of contrasts. I believe that this will allow the reader to see the connectivity between philosophy, their relative strategy, their tactical steps, including people selection, process needs and procedures. As a contrast, the book will cover:

- Toyota's Supply Chain and GM's Supply Chain
- The Supply Chain structure at each company
- The supplier working relationships at both organizations
- The leverages each company has with its Supply Chain
- Bottom line results

Besides the above, this book investigates the benefits & downfalls of key Supply Chain decisions, the logic necessary to make some counterintuitive solutions and how to tune your Supply Chain in your organization for specific results. The concept of Supplier Ecosystem is explored throughout the book with some key questions covered at the interview chapter in the end of the book.

During my several years in Industry, I have worked in Senior Management and Executive positions at General Motors, Parker Hannifin and Mahindra & Mahindra Ltd. I have had assignments at Toyota NUMMI, Shanghai GM and GM Korea.

Most of the information that is presented in this book, was a part of the research work done during my expat assignments in Asia. Based on a review of 200 suppliers in phase I, 36 in depth end-to-end reviews were conducted at key suppliers in phase II, with an equal mix of Toyota and General Motors suppliers in US and Asia. The data collected represents a 13.67% margin of error at a 90% confidence level for the sample. The results were the basis for the Supply Chain strategy implementation at three Asian plants. The performance results are included in the interview chapter and represent a high fidelity for the results.

One of the difficulties in this project, was the relative comparative measures, when you are dealing with two different supply chains. Instead of pursuing an elusive measure, the book presents some specialized tools for alternative stand-in measures. Examples of usage are included in the final chapter with the author's interview.

The book is based on research on Toyota, GM and their supply chains. But in real life, Honda and Toyota share many of the same Ecosystem concepts, and General Motors, Ford and FCA Chrysler share many of the elements of the cost margin model. Since the intent of this book is to peal the onion and contrast the working concepts, I have chosen two fictional companies, Toyonda Motors and Global Motors. Toyonda has an Ecosystem approach, and Global Motors has a Cost Margin model, just like their real-life counterparts. These models and their benefits & pitfalls will be detailed in the book.

While the book focusses on the supply chain in two specific companies, the intent of the book is not to show that one company's philosophy or process is better than the other. The specific benefits of each strategy and tactic are explored in the final chapter.

-The tale of two supply chains: Toyota and GM-

Supply Chain Management

Disclaimer

The information presented in this book is based on the research and experience of the author and his team, along with data gathered from public sources.

No proprietary information is included in this book, except where attributed to the data owner.

-The tale of two supply chains: Toyota and GM-

Supply Chain Management

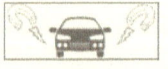

Premise

"The Tale of Two Supply Chains" follows the parallel story of two men, Steve and Kevin Radue, managing the Supply Chains at two fictional companies, Toyonda Motor Company and Global Motors Corporation. As identified earlier, Toyonda Motors supplier philosophy is based on the Supplier Ecosystem approach of the Supply Chain concept, the common elements demonstrated by Toyota Motor Co Asia operations, Honda Motors US Operations and Toyota Motor US Operations, while Global Motors is based on General Motors Corporation, Ford Motor Corporation and parts of Fiat Chrysler Automobiles US Operations.

Many of the details are a recreation of the Automaker's Supply Chain systems from supplier descriptions, surveys and supplier personnel accounts. It is the author's intent to demonstrate a range of Supply Chain strategies and their net results.

The author's personal modelling of Supply Chain and a transition plan for your business (automotive or other business) is covered in the final chapter. The discussion is to assist the reader navigate from one Supply Chain culture to another, through an ala carte of Supply Chain strategies.

The story is presented as a two person narrative, between Steve and Kevin. Each chapter focus on the story of one company, with Steve and Kevin taking turns to highlight their company strategies.

-The tale of two supply chains: Toyota and GM-

Supply Chain Management

-The tale of two supply chains: Toyota and GM-

Cast of Characters

Toyonda Corporation

- Bill Zemanski, VP and Lynn Gussett, his secretary
- Keith Takasaki, Regional Supply Chain manager
- Kevin Radue, Shukko
- Other Shukkos:
    - David Joseph (Supplier Development Manager)
    - Jonathan Edwards (Supplier Quality Manager)
    - Josh Herrera (Supplier Launch Manager)
- Kevin's initial team: Rebecca (Becky) Levy, Jason Nishi, Ralph Sygenda, Jack Fromm
- Tom Nakamura, Plant Manager, Mississippi Plant #1
- Jorge Westmont, Asst Plant Manager (Quality)
- Rob Gonzales, Logistics Coordinator

Kevin's family: Donna (spouse), Cameron and Carlie

Global Motors

- George Anderson, Senior VP Operations & Supply Chain
- Sammy Baker, Plant Manager, Ohio Plant
- Art Malik, Plant Manager, Ontario Plant
- Steven Radue, VP Purchasing
- Joel "JP" Olenzek, VP Marketing
- Jennifer Ming, Program Director
- Chuck Rainer, Supply Quality Director
- Sanjeev Kumar, Vehicle Line Executive

Steve's family: Debbie (spouse), Jake and Jordan

-The tale of two supply chains: Toyota and GM-

-The tale of two supply chains: Toyota and GM-

Chapter 1: Kevin's visit to the plant
August 31, Monday
Plant #1, Toyonda vehicle assembly, Mississippi

The first thing I notice when taking the interstate exit to the vehicle plant, is that the overflow production parking lot is completely full. Cars are parked in every available spot in the lot. Some are parked in the access road to the lot.

Something must be terribly wrong, I think to myself.

Car plants are well oiled machines, every day's production leaves the plant within 24 hours.

If the lot is full, something or someone screwed up outbound logistics. Or worse, something screwed up production.

I find a parking spot closest to the main offices of the plant. I use the small umbrella that I picked up at the airport this morning, as I run up the stairs to enter the building, folding the umbrella as I walk through the main door. It has been raining nonstop, since I reached the rental car counter at the Memphis airport, before the drive here.

"Hello Kevin, how was your trip in this morning."

I turn towards the voice and see the plant's front desk officer, as I am pushing the rickety turnstile to enter the building. I don't recognize him and strain my eyes to read his name tag.

"A bit of an early start today to fly here from Michigan. Billy Bob, is it? You must be new here. I don't think I have seen you here before." I say cheerfully trying not to bring the rain into the conversation.

"I started here last week. Getting used to it now." he says, keeping up the pleasantries.

-The tale of two supply chains: Toyota and GM-

"By the way, Bill's secretary left you a note to see him right away when you reach here."

"Bill Who. Bill Zemanski?", I say rather in disbelief.

"Yes, she said that he will be available after 8:30am."

I am surprised that Bill wants to see me. Bill is the VP of Supply Chain and he is mostly at the plant executive offices. He attends the monthly Executive Sourcing Forum, where the buyers present their purchasing recommendations. However, I have not interacted with him one on one.

If this is about the overflow of cars, then there is a production problem, somehow connected with the suppliers.

I check my watch for time. It is 7:55am.

Good, I can do some background checking before I head out to see him.

I head over to my transient desk to leave my briefcase. I am a Shukko, that is a Procurement Manager from the corporate office assigned to support the vehicle plants. One additional responsibility for the *Shukko* role is maintaining supplier relationships. So, I visit the plants and suppliers regularly to ensure that there are no open commercial issues and the supplier maintains their quality & delivery commitments to the Plant. My wife, Donna jokes that a Shukko is a fancy name for a road warrior.

I wear a dual time zone Charles-Hubert watch, that Donna gave me last Christmas. It is now set the US Central time and Japan time. I do keep myself connected to both sides of the pacific.

I call the Production manager and he does not answer. He must be in the plant floor and the cell phone reception is poor there. I log into the company's production schedule and see that the plant has worked substantial overtime over the last weekend.

If the plant has worked substantial overtime, but still not shipped cars, then either supplier quality or production quality is an issue.

Now it is time to meet with Bill. I decide to call his office, before I show up. I reach his secretary, Lynn.

"Good Morning Lynn", I say with a forced cheer.

"Good morning Kevin. How was your flight this morning?", she asks.

"Cramped flight, but no delays, even with the rain," I tell her. "Billy Bob at front desk said that Bill wanted to see me today. What is this about, Lynn?"

"I am not sure. But he is expecting you asap", she says. "Is there anything that I need to bring with me?" I ask still trying to get an understanding of the purpose of the meeting.

My mind is going through the scenarios, why cars were not shipped. Our team in Supply Chain has added 6 new suppliers in the past two quarters. *Could these suppliers have messed up production?* These suppliers represent a drop in the bucket compared to the existing incoming material at the plant.

Lynn's voice pulls me back into reality. "No just come by yourself. He wants to talk to you before your 9:00am team huddle," she says. "Keith is in the transit lounge in London airport and may join you by phone, if necessary," she continues.

Keith Takasaki is the Regional Supply Chain Manager, and my boss. His office is at the company's North American HQ in Michigan. Bill is Keith's boss and is the VP of Operations & Supply Chain.

-The tale of two supply chains: Toyota and GM-

I head to the elevator on my way to Bill's office. His office is on the top floor.

The first person you see when you enter Bill's office annex is Lynn at her desk. Lynn has the look of a librarian from a 1950s movie kind of way. Her glasses make her look sharp, and her desk is well organized. She is wearing a grey and white, long sleeved two-tone dress. She must be in her early 40s. Her wallboard has a mixture of post-its and colored checkmarks. Reminds me of a project tracker's office, not a secretary's office.

There is a picture of her dog, a black lab with a younger version of Lynn. Must be her daughter. There is a coffee mug on the shelf, that says "Yoda, the best secretary", next to the poster of Yoda's ten best quotes.

"Bill is ready for you," says Lynn looking

from her keyboard, as I walk in. She gets up and walks up to Bill's office door, knocking gently as she walks in. I follow her in.

"Can I get you'all some coffee?" Lynn asks Bill and me, smilingly. When we decline, she gets back to her desk.

Bill has a puff of grey hair, in the middle of his chestnut and black hair. He is in his late 40s, young among the Toyonda executives. He is at his desk, with rolled up sleeves looking through some charts.

Supply Chain Magazine ran a cover page story on him, that described him as a Strategic thinker, someone who rewrites supply chain rules by his actions. There are two boxes of cigars on the side table. I know that he loves his cigars; his cover shot has him enjoying a $500 Mayan Sicar Cigar.

The flush oak panelling in his office is a change of pace from the rest of the plant offices. His passion for vintage aeroplanes is visible in the office wall pictures. There are pictures of various old aircraft being restored, from a Wright brother's replica plane on one side to the Louis Bellot's model plane, the first to cross the English Channel. In the corner, I spot a picture of Bill standing next to Neil Armstrong.

Bill motions me to sit down. He looks at me solemnly.

"Good morning Bill," I say.

"Good morning Kevin. Hope you had a good flight in," he says. "You know the latest news from NHTSA. Our quality issues are on their radar," he starts. He cuts to the chase and does not take much time in chit chats.

"Yes", I nod. Our track record of defect free new product launches has taken a hit in the last year.

"I know, you are wondering why you are here in my office," he continues. "In the past six months, we have had two quality spills at the plant. In fact, the HVAC supplier just sent us a new quality alert this weekend."

"I do not know how bad the current situation is and if it is contained in the plant. You have worked with these suppliers for the past 18 months preparing for their launch. What is your honest opinion of these new suppliers?" he asks pensively.

"For most part these new suppliers are very responsive. I have worked with these suppliers in their commercial agreements. Not much on the technical side. However, I did not see any problems," I say, with my eyes looking up as I try to recollect if there were any warning signs.

"Fair enough. I am concerned on their track record for quality. This time, we have worked a full weekend of overtime and still have a backlog of non-saleable vehicles," he says.

"Since Keith's expat assignment is ending in a few weeks, I want you to lead and report back to me," he adds.

"We have had a full weekend of overtime and we have not caught up with production," he repeats for emphasis.

I can't help but gasp at that overtime. *A full weekend of overtime and the production vehicles are still not ready to ship out of the plant.*

"I will investigate and lead the supplier kaizen response," I say to Bill pensively, trying to get a feel of the magnitude of the task ahead of me.

"This vehicle launch is a crucial testament to our new supplier strategy. I need a daily progress report," says Bill.

As I walk out, I tell him that I had known Neil, when I was at Purdue.

"Neil was a Purdue football fan. My brother was in the Engineering school and knew him well," I say.

"You played football at Purdue. Did you meet him at the field?" asks Bill.

"Yes, he made it to a handful of games every year. I remember one time, the band director took the band quartet and few of us, the players to surprise Neil with an impromptu song show, for his 60th birthday," I add.

"That must have been a great experience", says Bill being impressed. Bill wraps up our conversation with some quick one-liners about his experience meeting Neil at the 40th anniversary celebration of the moon landing.

As I walk out of Bill's office, I reflect on the assignment that he has given me. It requires working with many suppliers, advocating, problem solving and managing change with the suppliers. It is the biggest assignment of my career. *Am I ready for it?*

Back at my desk, I am getting the Purchasing team ready for the weekly huddle. Our buyer team had people from various backgrounds. Becky was a college intern before her work here. Jack and Ralph were Assembly techs and rose through the ranks, with the college benefits offered at work. When I had joined the team, each person was new to the company and I had to spend a good part of the first year mentoring them on the purchasing process.

I remember Steve Job describing his first business team, that each member was like a rough-cut gem. Work at Apple had shaped them like a rock tumbler into precious stones. My team is the same way now. I can't imagine now doing my job without them. We cover for each other seamlessly, since we travel out of town for supplier visits quite often. Jason has just joined the team as the new college intern. My team supports sourcing & logistics and is located at the plant.

I pick up my laptop and get ready for the team huddle. We work closely with three other Shukkos and they join us in the huddle. David Joseph is responsible for Supplier Development, Jonathan Edwards for Supplier Quality and Josh Herrera for Supplier Launch. It is the first time in two weeks that we are all meeting face to face. After a brief catch up, we get started. I describe my meeting with Bill Zemanski. "Bill was very clear that the quality alerts are out of control with the new suppliers. He wants a daily progress report, until a corrective action is in place," I summarize Bill's expectation.

"One whole weekend. That is over one hundred thousand dollars in just wages," says Josh. "High price," adds Jonathan. I pause for a moment to let the impact settle in.

"The first step is understanding the reasons for the overtime," says David.

I nod in agreement.

"How is the quality issue connected to the plant overtime?" asks Jason. I am glad that my team is looking beyond the sourcing issues to understand the plant problem.

"Good question. We need to discuss this with the quality manager to understand the issue," I say.

The other Shukkos nod in agreement and I dial the Plant Manager to see if we can get the reports for this past week. The plant manager's secretary, Brenda-Lou tells us that he is tied up in a meeting. Instead, she will connect us to Jorge Westmont, the Assistant Plant Manager. Jorge is the head of plant quality as well.

"Good morning Kevin," says Jorge.

"Good morning Jorge", I say, glad that I have reached the head of quality, to get the background on this quality issue.

"Jorge, I heard that you are off-site. But I just found out about the quality concern at the plant from the last weekend and I am trying to collect all the details," I continue.

"Our quality and overtime are out of control," starts Jorge, with a rather gloomy assessment. However, he is very animated in explaining the issue to us.

"This past week's overtime is just the tip of the iceberg", he says. "We have several hours of overtime for the past 3 weeks."

The situation is more dire than I thought. If the problem has not been escalated to me and not been solved by the plant quality in the last 3 weeks, then this month is going to look terrible financially.

"There are 6 suppliers that have caused most of the issues for us," Jorge adds. "I will email that list asap to you. Please review the details and let's meet face to face tomorrow morning, when I am back at the plant".

"Your team was responsible for developing these suppliers. I expect you to fix this issue," he says bluntly.

We end the call, with Jorge agreeing to send me the list of issues in the last 3 weeks along with the A3 problem-solving sheets that his team has worked so far. By the time, the conference call ends there is an email in my inbox.

From: Westmont, Jorge
Sent: August 31, 10:35 AM
To: Radue, Kevin
Cc: Joseph, David; Edwards, Jonathan; Herrera, Josh; Levy, Rebecca; Nishi, Jason; Sygenda, Ralph; Fromm, Jack
Subject: JIT and incoming quality issues at Plant #1

Hello Kevin:

Enclosed is the production run schedule for the past 3 weeks.

Week of		Mon	Tue	Wed	Thurs	Fri	Sat	Total
Aug-23	Hours	16	16	16+2	16+2	16+2	10	96
	VPD	1152	1,036	948	950	920	680	5686
Aug-16	Hours	16	16	16+2	16+2	16	8	92
	VPD	1036	1152	1152	948	980	520	
Aug-09	Hours	16	16	16	16	16+2	0	82
	VPD	1152	1152	1152	1036	1024	0	5516

Total expectation of vehicles per day (VPD): 1152

The prior week we made the production in the scheduled hours with no overtime.

-The tale of two supply chains: Toyota and GM-

The Pareto of supplier issues is:

1. HVAC systems - Brazing issue - 8 stoppages
2. Seat JIT schedule issue - 4 stoppages
3. Radiator weld issue - 4 stoppages
4. Front steering bolt failure - 1 stoppage
5. Improper Tire issue - 1 stoppage
6. Improper trunk latch - 1 stoppage

Product engineers are aware of these issues. Please discuss this with them for further details.

-Jorge Westmont
Assistant Plant Manager
Mississippi Plant #1

"I am confused what the problem is" says Jason Nishi. "I thought Bill was concerned about quality, but this email is about overtime."

"You are right," I say. "But the problem is really two-fold. It is quality, but the first indicator is overtime."

"I don't follow" says Jason with a quizzical look on his face.

"You know that the plant has a takt time of 50 seconds, that means that there is a new car produced every 50 seconds," I say.

"If the quality issues delay the line due to stoppages, then Jorge has to plan for 30 extra hours to make up the shortfall of 2000 cars and catch up on production," says Becky. "The overtime is due to slow production and line shutdowns caused by unacceptable incoming quality," adds Jack.

"Now if the plant's final inspection has not approved the outbound shipment, then we have 2000 extra cars in the overflow production lot, not ready for sale. That is even more painful," I continue.

"Is every week perfect with no overtime?" asks Jason surprised.

"A typical week will have about 5 hour or less of total overtime. For every hour of downtime, the plant loses 65 units of production" I say.

"The plant encourages assembly techs to stop the line if they observe a defect that they can't fix in their station. But perennial overtime is a symptom of a deeper problem," adds David.

After that horrible surprise, I look up to restart the conversation on our next steps.

"Ralph, you are the buyer for the HVAC. Was there anything on the radar for this supplier that could indicate this problem?"

"The HVAC system is a new greenfield supplier. But their pre-production run had no hiccups," says Ralph, rather defensively.

"Their pre-production track history is not going to get us very far," adds Becky.

"Ralph you have to lead the Kaizen at the supplier plant. Can you discuss with product engineering and the Shukkos to see who can support you on this?" I add.

Our purchasing team is responsible for vehicle trim, so our team will take the lead on most issues. We end the meeting agreeing to divide up the supply base problems between our teams.

- Ralph - HVAC systems
- Becky – Seats, in conjunction with Jonathan
- Me - Coordinate report out from Powertrain team on Radiator, commodities from other purchasing teams
- Jack - Tires, latch, Steering bolt
- Me - Overall report out

- Other Shukkos – Support for leading quality reviews

We agree that we will report out at a roundup meeting at 3pm every day. It is going to be a busy course for a few weeks. I see a lot of travel and late nights. But I am glad that the assignments match the areas of purchasing responsibility. Each person has a load to carry, if we can pull out of this quality slump now.

We wrap up and head to our desks to make some calls to get the ball rolling. After lunch and several supplier calls, I look at my watch. It is time for our first roundup meeting.

I walk into the conference room at 3pm. All the other team members are already there. Jonathan Edwards, the Supplier Quality Team leader begins the meeting to get us up to speed on his supplier, Lear Seating. The supplier has hired a new transportation company for delivering seats just in time for production. Toyonda electronically publishes its build schedule to its supplier.

Lear plant is about 80 miles away and builds and ships seats in the same sequence to be delivered to the plant, two hours before the build. The incoming seat colors and trim levels match the build sequence. The seating is delivered right to the assembly line. In this case, the transportation logistics operator picked up a wrong batch of seats for delivery.

"How is it possible to have the same mistake four times?" I ask. "If it is four times, then it is a systemic issue, not an oversight."

There was a manifesto process gap between Lear and the transportation company. The date field in their SAP interface, was associated with the wrong order. Jonathan assures that the team is looking into the electronic issue. Meanwhile, they have gone to paper copy and manual signoff to continue the production. The cross functional team will be on site to review the issue and work with the transportation company to ensure smooth correction. The ability to work directly with the Tier-2 to solve problems is a hallmark of our company. Jonathan will travel to Lear for coordinating their onsite problem solving and to further understand the working issues.

Ralph from my team will travel to the HVAC supplier tomorrow. The quality engineers will be there as well. We finish the team meeting and I type up a quick note to Bill to keep him in the loop. He will want to know the issues, since this is the first time, we have had such a substantial quality issue at Toyonda.

The rest of the day is a blur with calls and collecting information. Today, we have just scratched the surface on two of the six quality issues. I look at my watch, it is just past 6pm.

There is a missed call from home. Donna has gone to visit her sister with the kids. The week after next week is the start of school, and this is the end of the summer for the kids. I haven't spoken to her all day, since I hurried to the airport this morning.

I give her a quick call.

"Hi honey, how was your day?" I open the conversation.

Donna sounds like she is in good spirits and the kids are having a good time. The kids went camping today and will be back tomorrow.

She reminds me to call the homeowners association for this weekend. "The kids would love to have the pool party at the club house," she says.

I assure her that I will. The weekend after is the Labor Day. It is also Carlie's birthday on that Saturday. We will have a pool party for the kids on Saturday and the family Labor Day bar-beque on Monday. We wrap up the call and I head out of the office.

By the time I reach the hotel it is late. It has been a long day from the flight in this morning to the late evening dinner at the hotel restaurant.

I have a full agenda tomorrow with suppliers and solving per Bill's request.

Chapter 2: Kevin's findings
September 1, Tuesday
Plant #1, Toyonda vehicle assembly, Mississippi

It is early in the morning as I pull into the plant office. I am still sipping the Starbucks coffee from the hotel breakfast. I see the employee parking lot is filled up; the first shift started about two hours ago.

The plant sits off the interstate in Mississippi on a land over 1200 acres. There are more than 8000 team members and 400 temp workers, besides about 800 supplier personnel. There are two separate assembly lines making about 2000 vehicles between the Car and SUV production lines. When the plant opened, many of the workers relocated here from the nearby cities such as Memphis.

I head to the plant entrance, rather than the office entrance and head straight to Jorge's office. Jorge has two offices; he is mostly at the plant office, a modular space on the mezzanine, rather than the well-furnished office at the executive floor. I walk into Jorge's office.

The supplier engineer is waiting for me. I agreed to meet with him since Ralph is at the supplier site.

"Good morning Jose," I say smiling, gracious that the supplier has flown in, on such a short notice.

Jose is in his mid-twenties. He is a big guy, from our HVAC supplier, located in Ramos Arizpe, just south of the border. He is wearing a hardhat and a reflective safety jacket. His forehead is little sweaty from walking up and down the narrow steps leading to the plant mezzanine offices. Jorge is nowhere to be seen.

"Good morning, Kevin" says Jose, turning around to see me.

It was a long day yesterday, so I make my second coffee as we head to the conference area on one side of Jorge's office.

"When did you come in?" I ask surprised since most flights from Mexico come in around noon to the Memphis airport.

"I flew in yesterday. I came asap so that I can collect data at our JIT staging warehouse, about a half hour from here," he says. Many suppliers have an assembly facility within an hour drive from the plant, so that they can coordinate the Just in Time – JIT deliveries to the plant.

"So, what have you found so far?" I ask.

"I have started the investigation on the failure data with the warehouse team," he says. "We reviewed all the production output from the past week. There is three day's supply of material at the plant. We have been able to quarantine all the defective units."

"That is great. Quarantine is the first action. Have you found the root cause?" I ask.

"Not yet. But we have eliminated six of the nine possibilities," he says briskly.

"Is there an 8D problem solving process at your site?" I ask quizzically.

"We will setup an 8D team shortly," he says.

Is the supplier walking through a step by step problem solving process, I think to myself. *I have been bitten before by suppliers jumping to improper conclusions and not following process.*

"Jose, quarantine is for interim corrective action and this is a major step. But, please review the 8D with the supplier quality engineer," I say.

8 disciplines or 8D is a structured problem-solving method covering eight steps. The steps start with getting the right people into a team to root causing and ending with interim and permanent corrective action, all the while validating that proposed solution is working. Many companies skip these steps especially the last two steps, that are how to prevent recurrence and closure documentation.

"The Kaizen team has identified some details for further review," says Jose.

"What have you found so far?" I ask.

"There is a fixture problem in the welding operation. And this is confirmed with Engineering," Jose explains.

"Excellent. Have you tested the solution?" I ask.

Jose explains the ongoing trials and it will take two days to complete the solution testing.

"You know that Toyonda expects a thorough 8D solution before resuming shipment. The only exception for temporary production is using parts with full inspection," I say. "You can begin shipment, if you have 100% inspection of all shippable parts."

Jorge just then walks back to the office. He had an early morning report-out meeting with the Plant Manager about the situation.

Jorge is a silver haired, middle aged plant executive, who has led the plant through the 10 years, since the plant started up here. He looks like the older version of actor Javier Bardem, right up to the unique haircut, in the Oscar winning movie, No Country for Old Men.

"Jose is making progress with quality issue identification. But I am concerned at the pace of solutions," I tell him.

Then I turn to Jose and tell him, "We need to get a production solution quickly or you will shut the plant down."

Jose describes a light screen station, that checks incoming parts, so that no parts miss the inline pressure check. "We can catch a poor weld, if there is a hole causing pressure leak," he says. The quality team at his company is testing good parts as "GO" samples and bad parts as "NO-GO" samples.

Jose reviews the documents with Jorge and me. Jorge asks him about various problem-solving tools. Jose shows his power point slide with a fault tree. He explains that the fault tree has considered all failure possibilities. He explains to Jorge that the supplier's initial diagnosis is that the parts missed the pressure test after welding. He is talking about installing a light screen after welding process to ensure that each part goes through the pressure check evaluation for weld continuity.

"Has the fault tree been reviewed with Engineering," Jorge asks Jose.

"Yes. We had a call yesterday to review it," says Jose.

It is my job to work with the supplier and Engineering to ensure that problems are solved. While the product engineer ensures the technical details are correct, I am responsible for the supplier relationship and ensuring that the supplier is on top of the details.

Jose unrolls his drawing and an A3 problem solving sheet. This A3 sheet is a typical collection of problem-solving steps that is recommended by our Japan HQ team. He shows me a picture of the weld issue.

I turn to Jorge and ask him, "How many vehicles are quarantined for this potential defect?"

Jorge opens his spreadsheet and checks for the numbers. "75 vehicles are suspect in that lot" he says.

The tale of two supply chains: Toyota and GM

"Can this problem be checked in the vehicle?" asks Jorge, looking at Jose.

Jose confirms that product development has tested a method of pressure checking in the installed vehicle.

"Then, lets meet in the quarantine lot at 11am". I tell Jose and head out to meet the new supplier, Vibramat Ltd.

As I head through the plant towards the office conference room, I can see the big stamping presses at work.

The steel coils enter the northern gates of the plant. Eight 100-ton presses blank out stampings for every vehicle body and structural component of the vehicle. The stamping presses look like a giant King Kong stomping its foot and causing the land to shudder. These machines consume 30 tons of steel every 30 minutes. It is a sight to see, raw coils entering on the north, being stamped into finished chassis and vehicle structures in a sequence of progressive dies. These structures are then moved to robotic welders that create the intricate shapes required for a car body and frame. A car body is made of more than 200 sheet metal parts welded together.

The next meeting with Vibramat, the plant finance and IT teams goes well. The supplier can adapt his electronic data exchange software to accept purchase orders from Toyonda. The supplier can also accept payments, production schedules and quality information from the plant database. Many of the US suppliers use a standard interface, Cognizant for data sharing and so Toyonda's system requires some additional programming for interface. This is the first good news that I have got on my trip here.

At 11am, I am at the plant quarantine lot. I meet up with Jose.

-The tale of two supply chains: Toyota and GM-

"Kevin, Let me get you caught up on our progress so far," says Jose. "Jorge gave me a list of VIN numbers and I have approval from Engineering to pressure test in the vehicle".

"Good progress," I say. "What time did you start the testing?"

"We started at 9am, and with a team of 5 Engineers, we have identified and tested 10 of the 75 suspect cars. We have been able to clear all 10 cars."

Jose then demonstrates the testing in one of the cars.

"So, once you locate the vehicle, it takes only 10 minutes to complete the test", I summarize. "Sounds like you have a working procedure for testing."

Jose and team continue the testing, while I take some supplier calls, as I am waiting in the lot.

By 1pm, Jose comes back to me. By this time, Jorge has joined us at the marshalling yard.

"I have some final results for you," he says. "We have tested 73 suspect vehicles and 27 vehicles either do not pass or need additional rework".

"What happened to the two other vehicles," I ask.

"Our teams are scouring the yard, but so far cannot locate those two vehicles," he says.

Jorge walks with Jose to find the two missing vehicles.

29 vehicles may have to be scrapped. *Oh God, that is a million dollars of inventory.*

The marshalling yard is starting to get busy. The East bound train is loading cars for shipment to the dealers. The westbound train arrives in the evening.

Jorge returns with the news that the two other cars were found and failed testing. He confirms that all the 29 vehicles have been quarantined.

"Is there any scrap or quarantine for the other quality issues?" I ask Jorge. He shakes his head, no.

Heading back, to the Executive offices, I meet up with Bill. I walk into his office to deliver the bad news. Bill is not happy but agrees with the decision to scrap the suspect cars. Toyonda philosophy is to overdeliver on quality, even in cases where the parts are suspect.

It is 2pm by the time I am done with the plant. I get into my rental car on the way to the airport.

This trip has been two long ... long days. Last night, I left the plant at 9pm. Today is a little shorter, since I am headed over to the airport to catch my flight back.

I pick-up my phone to call Donna as I wait to drop off the car. The next two days are going to be hectic in dealing with suppliers.

-The tale of two supply chains: Toyota and GM-

Supply Chain Management

Chapter 3: Kevin and supply chain problem solving
September 3, Thursday
Toyonda Corporation HQ Building, Michigan

It is Thursday morning. I am driving to the Toyonda Corporation headquarters, my base office.

The Toyonda North America R&D headquarters building and the Engineering Center are set in a 100 acre site in Southeast Michigan. As you pull off the highway, nothing is visible for a few hundred yards. Just past the hill, you would see the entire campus with the glass building for the headquarters, two white buildings that comprise the Engineering Center and the prototype lab, along with a criss-cross of test tracks at the back of the property. The area is rather spread out, but it is hard to imagine that there are more than 6000 people on site here.

Yesterday, I had visited the Vibramat supplier site to evaluate their facility as a new supplier. Today was the first day back at the office.

It is quarter past six as I head to the elevator and on to the second floor. I like the "early shift", when I am at the Headquarters. Early US time is late in Japan, but my counterparts in Japan work the late shift, so that we can have some common time.

We work as a team on most commodities, with all sourcing recommendations done at the purchasing manager level.

Another bonus of an early schedule is that it helps me to beat the rush hour traffic both ways and get home in the evening at a decent hour and spend time with my family. Donna and the kids will be returning home today, after visiting her sister. And this weekend is Carlie's birthday, my youngest kid, just before she starts first grade next Tuesday.

-The tale of two supply chains: Toyota and GM-

I turn on my computer and glance at my notes from my trip. Ralph, Becky, Jack and Jonathan have sent me their notes and preliminary 8Ds report from the quality review on Monday. I plan to summarize these details in my daily report out to Bill and my trip report to Keith.

I have a meeting with Keith at 8am. Keith has been a good boss and mentor for me. He recruited me from college 8 years ago and was patient with me as I learned the ropes of the Toyonda Supply Chain. He has a calm demeanor and a balanced perspective, even in tough situations, with a sternness and a smile always on his face. Keith is tall at 6 ft. He reminds me of Tom Selleck, in the 1980s TV show, Magnum PI.

I knock at Keith's door, exactly at 7:59am. I know that Keith values punctuality to a dot. He motions me to come in.

As I walk in, I notice that Keith is not his usual self. His face is tensed, and he is busy pouring over a stack of papers and he is on the phone. He motions me with a finger up, asking me to hold for a minute as he wraps up his call. It is 8am and he ends his call and starts with me.

"G'morning Kevin"

"Good morning Keith. How are you. I heard from Bill that you are wrapping up your expat term," I say.

"Yes. All good things must come to an end," he says quickly. "However, we are in the middle of the supplier localization drive and I will support this through, whether I am here or back at the home country."

"How was your plant and supplier visit?" Keith asks about the details of my trip.

Keith is methodical, I think to myself. *The supplier review with Vibramat was the main purpose of my trip, although tackling the last-minute quality issue was par for the course. Still these reviews and closure of the open quality concerns are a part of Toyonda's localization strategy.*

"This new supplier is a current supplier for Ford and Fiat Chrysler today. Their quality tech score and finances look good. Everything else looks ready for the delivery of functional samples," I say, summarizing my meeting at the plant and the visit to their site.

"And what makes up their good tech score?" he asks quizzically.

"Our supplier audit teams has rated their quality tracking and problem-solving process areas as good. All returned parts from their current programs are root caused and any corrections are implemented in their parts to all the automakers," I say describing their background for achieving a good technical capability score.

"What about their finances? Any leverage?" he asks delving further into their background.

"Yes, some," I say, and I pull out the Vibramat file to get the specifics on their debt. Many new suppliers use debt to get their operations ready before they go out for new business, which in turn hurts them with not enough operating cash for driving the new business.

"Has their leverage level been approved by the Supplier Audit team?" he asks. Their debt to equity is close to 50%, a little on the high side. I admit that they are still under review.

"What is the vehicle plant's take on the supplier?" he continues.

"The supplier plant is located 100 miles away. So, this would require that the plant pickup daily shipment through Lightfoot transport," I explain.

Lightfoot transport is Toyonda's third party logistics company. The Toyonda Supply Chain concept is that most inbound materials are shipped free on board, FOB, from the supplier plant. The plant logistics manages the material from the arrival timing and cross-docking to the material unpack schedule and when the material reaches the assembly line; All from A to Z.

"Product engineers and supplier development have approved the quality of the initial appearance samples. The next step is getting functional samples," I say explaining their current status.

"That's good. So, you have one more supplier that is in progress to make our plan," he says summarizing the situation. "How is the overall status of the localization plan?"

"In the first phase, as you know, we brought in 6 new suppliers. Now we are looking at 10 new suppliers for the next phase. That will take us to 32% of the supply base, including the start-up suppliers. However, only 2 of the 10 suppliers have been approved so far," I say summing up.

"Compared to our plan, we are 6 months behind on finding the right suppliers," he adds. I nod with a sigh, as we move on to the more pressing plant issue from my meeting with Bill.

"How was the quality issue at the plant? What happened?" he asks.

"Today, we have completed the quarantine of all defective parts at the plant. No customer vehicles are affected. All 6 kaizen groups have identified a permanent corrective action, that is being tested," I tell him, summarizing the trip. "I know that you are caught up with the side details through email CCs with Bill."

"Scrap cost is high. We have 29 vehicles for HVAC and about 2 other vehicles for other defects. All these cars will be scrapped," I add.

"I have looked at Jorge's email from Monday," Keith asks with a pensive glance. "I know that you are working with the kaizen teams to solve the supplier quality issues. Do you see any similarities in the issues between the suppliers?"

"Two of the 6 suppliers had brazing or welding problems," I say stating the obvious.

"Yes...." he says.

"So brazing is a complex process that suppliers are struggling to have consistent quality," I say. "I have asked David and the Supplier quality team to evaluate each supplier's brazing and welding quality before supplier's win new business."

"That is a good start," he says.

I see that Keith is disappointed that I could not see anything more in the situation and from Jorge's notes.

"I am sure that the team and you are going to solve the current quality problems," he says finally.

"But have you checked if these problems have a similar root cause, besides brazing and other old school technology. What will you do to eliminate this type of issues in the future?" he asks reflectively.

I am confused. *How can six different suppliers with different products have similarities in quality issues. What can we do to solve these?*

Looking at my quizzical look, he adds "Check up on their supplier performance metrics during their production ramp-up."

I haven't looked for similarities among different supplier problems. "I will get back to you," I say to park the issue while I research the next steps.

"We expected start up hiccups," I say. "but not at this level".

"One thing we have to ensure is good process," says Keith.

"Remember, the Detroit's big three choose suppliers based on the lowest cost bidder, but our strategy is to choose the best supplier. Working on their product cost comes a close second," he says contrasting us to our cross-town counterparts.

"Our Ecosystem approach maintains a 90 to 95% supplier retention, compared to the local automakers who retain about 60% of the suppliers for every subsequent model," he adds.

"There are about 100 supplier engineers at our facility here to ensure product synergy, while we launch new vehicles," he says further explaining the differences.

"How does a Ford or Fiat-Chrysler handle this many?" I ask curiously.

"Typically, there may be a handful of resident supplier engineers there," he says. "But all of this, is to manage supplier design and the product cost after their supplier selection, not before," he adds.

Keith leans over his desk and looks at me.

"You remember our discussion on continuous learning as a key element in supply chain guiding philosophy?" he asks. "That learning element of the Supply Chain is not working," he adds softly.

"What do you mean ..... suppliers are not learning?" I ask being puzzled.

"The suppliers do not have an opportunity to learn," he says. "In the Asian plants, the larger suppliers teach the smaller suppliers. But here it is not working," he adds.

"Why would the larger suppliers teach other suppliers?" I ask quizzically. "If the parts are procured from a system aggregator kind of supplier, they will have to work with their tier 2 and tier 3 levels for maintaining the quality," he says.

"So, in Asia we buy only full systems from suppliers that are system aggregator?" I say with a surprise. "Yes. That can be mostly true. And the quality development process flows downhill," he summarizes the strategy.

"How do you create a Supply Chain level learning when all the suppliers are independent?" I ask trying to contrast the current situation.

"That is a great question. We have to solve that first for our Supply Chain network to grow," he says as a aha moment.

It is 10 am, we wrap up and I need to hurry to my next meeting. The next two meetings go quickly.

At 11:30am, I catch a break between meetings. I must review my new supplier plan. There are several new suppliers that we are planning for the supplier review in upcoming phases of localization. I review the files that my buyers have put together for their supplier recommendation.

I pull up Becky's file and her recommendation for a new component sourcing. All three suppliers are small to midsize companies. But each has a substantially different quality history.

1. Chicago Steel - Quality rating 75/100 (Below Average)
2. Musui - Quality rating 90/100 (Acceptable)
3. Korensa - Quality rating 82/100 (Acceptable)

I call Becky to review the supplier recommendation.

"G' Morning Becky. How are you this morning?" I ask. "Good Morning Kevin," she says.

"Any plans for the upcoming long weekend," I ask. "Planning to have some me-time. I will meet up with some friends on Saturday. But hope to curl up with a good book the rest of the weekend," she says. "How about you?"

"My brother, Steve and his family will be at my place. We plan to have a Labor Day get together," I say about my plans for the long weekend.

-The tale of two supply chains: Toyota and GM-

"On your supplier recommendation, I see that one supplier is below average and the other two are acceptable for quality. Do you have a tech score for them as well?" I ask enquiringly.

"Supplier development has graded Korensa at 72 out of 100, and Musui as 87 for their tech scores. Tell me, I never really understood why we have a quality score and a technical score?" she asks inquisitively.

"A quality score is an absolute cut-off. If the supplier has a score below the cut-off, we can't source to them, until they bring the score up to the target," I explain. "However, a tech score is a rating of how well a supplier is expected to perform. So, a good supplier will have a better score than an average supplier."

"In your case, Korensa is average and Musui is a high performer, based on their tech scores" I summarize.

"What does that mean?" she asks. "Let us review their quotes and then we can discuss the tech score effect on their quotes," I say.

"Between Musui and Korensa, there is a substantial difference in cost. Musui has a $28.20 quote versus a $26.10 at Korensa, both will be FOB cost at the supplier within 50 miles from the plant," she says explaining the quotes.

"That is good. A supplier with a good tech score, will be able to deliver on the cost to the program much better than a supplier that is competing only on cost," I explain.

"So how do I compare suppliers?" she asks to clarify how to proceed.

"A ten-point difference in technical score says that the supplier has better R&D facilities, more mature supply chain processes, product innovations in the pipeline and a quick turnaround in production issue resolution," I say. "I would present this as a 10% cost change in year one and an additional 5% in year two. That is my rule of thumb."

-The tale of two supply chains: Toyota and GM-

"So how do I execute it?" she asks. "You should propose a cost down path with the supplier and agree on a plan. Anything over on top of the plan can be shared with the supplier," I say categorically.

"Interesting. Let me discuss this with the supplier and get back to you," she says finally.

"Let them know, the better they perform now, the better their chances of getting our future business, since they get into our supplier ecosystem," I say to encourage her discussion.

We wrap up the call

I leave office at 3pm and get home. Donna is home by the time, I reach home. Carlie runs up to the door.

"Hello Daddy. Did you miss me?" she asks.

"Hello Sweetheart," I say. "I missed you so much" and pick her up with a big hug.

"What are you getting me for my birthday?" she asks, thinking forward to the weekend.

"Can I get a pony?" she asks.

"We got to check with Mommy," trying to deflect an immediate answer.

"Why not?" says Donna, while winking at me.

I smile and tell her about the pool party that we have planned for her. Her cousins and friends will be there.

Saturday is finally here. Carlie is excited about her birthday party that evening. My brother, Steve and his family came home just after lunch to join us. His kids, Jake and Jordan play XBOX with my son, Cameron upstairs.

-The tale of two supply chains: Toyota and GM-

Steve is the VP of Purchasing at Global Motors. We have been competitive between us, since our kindergarten days. Steve is about 6 years older than me, in his early 40s. Donna is good friends with Steve's wife, Debbie. Steve and I never really talk about work, more out of our mutual competitiveness.

By noon time, the decorations are up at the clubhouse. Donna had organized pony rides, swimming pool lifeguards and a magic show. The birthday party is a grand hit. The clown did many tricks and Callie and her friends were having a good time. I see ponies dressed up with fake unicorn horns is a big hit with the younger kids.

Donna had organized an Xbox party for the teens as well. The party ends at 7pm. It is 8pm before the last parent picks up their kids.

Labor Day barbeque is a similar hit. Steve had brought some venison and alligator meat. The charcoal flavour to the Venison steak had kids and adults scrambling for seconds. He brought 20 lbs of Venison, and it was all gone in a short time.

It is 5pm by the time, I open a bottle of wine to catch up with Steve to find out how he is doing. We gather in the study to listen to some music with the wine.

As I open the wine as I wonder how the Supply Chain culture is at Global Motors and what kinds of challenges does Steve have in his day to day.

Does he deal with similar issues? Is his supply chain structure more strategic or tactical than at Toyonda?

Steve and I have always been close since our parents passed away when I was in high school. While we talk about everything else, we have kept our work experiences separate.

Chapter 4: Steve's Dilemma
September 8, Tuesday
Global Motors HQ

It is 830am. George Anderson's staff meeting at the 11th floor of the Global Motors headquarters had just wrapped up. I was walking out in a daze. George's prediction was very clear. The midsize platform was not going to be profitable this year. This would create a major issue in profitability for the whole company.

I am Steven Radue, the VP for Worldwide Purchasing at Global Motors. George is my boss, the Senior VP and the head of all plant operations.

This midsize platform, internally known as the C- platform is the highest volume segment and a loss like this is a huge business risk for the company. Granted that the market was tough this year, with several new competitor entries. Each new vehicle had some unique feature, drawing away new customers and had split the market.

I reach out to take some Tylenol, to relieve the massive headache coming up. The pain started from my back and came up through my spine, spreading quickly like fire. It is as if, I had been jabbed with a million needles from my neck down. Each needle was dabbed in alcohol to numb the pain, but I can feel each pin hole.

I must get to the bottom of this, I think to myself, *or we will be in deep trouble. If we don't fix this, Global Motors may one day have to discontinue small car production and stick to SUVs and trucks.*

The C-car platform is the most popular industry segment, with competitors ranging from the Ford Fusion and the Hyundai Sonata in cars, to Honda CRV and the Nissan Murano in small SUVs. My thoughts were interrupted only by my buzzing iPhone. I got a new phone last weekend, and the company's Corporate portal installation had locked it up. So, it has been annoying me with a notification buzz every few minutes this morning.

Heading back to my office, I stop at Janet's desk. Janet is my secretary. She is a model of efficiency. Sometimes, I feel that she can run the whole place, especially when I travel out of office, such as I was last week. Janet is busy printing the winner announcement for the Labor Day weekend Annual Chili cookoff competition from last weekend.

"Good morning, Janet, how was the competition last week?" I ask.

"Good morning, Steve," she says with a smile. And she quickly adds "It was the best chili so far. Too bad you missed it."

"Not so bad," I tell her. "Joe sent us some of his chili home. The kids enjoyed it. Did he win this year too?". Joe lives down the street and won the Master Chili Chef award at the last year's competition.

"Joe came in third this year. The competition was fierce" says Janet.

"I am glad it was a success," I say approvingly.

"By the way, here are my notes from George's staff meeting. Please scan them into One Notes so that I can show them to my staff. Another thing Janet, my new iPhone has been buzzing all morning. It is driving me nuts. Can you talk to IT?" I add. I leave her my phone and my notes as I head to my office.

At my desk, I open my laptop. The first email is from Sanjeev, the Vehicle Line executive. Sanjeev had presented the profitability details at George's meeting. Our C platform has four vehicle models, code named, CDX40 and CJX50 for the two cars and MDY200 and MYJ300 for the SUV & truck. Things were not very rosy for the platform.

From: Kumar, Sajeev
Sent: September 8, 9:32AM

-The tale of two supply chains: Toyota and GM-

To: George Anderson's Staff

Enclosed is the material from today's staff meeting. The concern is that the breakeven volume targets must be adjusted to meet market conditions. Long term profitability is at risk.

Cost Analysis (in thousands)

Capital investment:	$450,080
Plant tool up (revenue budget allocation):	$150,020
Supplier tool up (revenue allocation):	$250,000
Product development and Test rollup:	$80,100
Plant upgrades:	$100,040

- Quick changeover tools
- Paint booth upgrade
- Railyard upgrade
- Plant test track upgrade

Total investment	$1,030,240

Cost allocation (in thousands)

1. CDX40 (20%), Breakeven at 550000 cars: $206,048
2. CJX50 (20%), Breakeven at 650,000 cars: $206,048
3. MDY200 (30%), Breakeven at 500,000 SUVs: $309,072
4. MYJ300 (30%), Breakeven at 625,000 Trucks: $309,072

Revised breakdown due to higher sales incentives

Cost allocation (in thousands)

1. CDX40, Breakeven at 685,000 cars
2. CJX50, Breakeven at 765,000 cars
3. MDY200, Breakeven at 500,000 SUVs
4. MYJ300, Breakeven at 625,000 Trucks

-The tale of two supply chains: Toyota and GM-

As you can see, per our sales trends we will not meet breakeven in the CDX40 and CJX50. I look for your opinions, if there are any opportunities to improve the breakeven through any other means.

-Sanjeev Kumar
Vehicle Line Executive

Reaching for my desk phone, I dial Sanjeev's number.

"Good Morning Sanjeev", I say and start the conversation. "Good Morning Steve. How are you doing? I was expecting your call," says Sanjeev.

"I need to understand the numbers better," I ask. "When are you available to meet?".

"I can meet you in 15 minutes at your office," says Sanjeev.

Shortly there is a gentle knock on the door and Sanjeev walks in. He has a laptop on one hand and three binders on the other hand. Sanjeev has steely gray hair that matches his steely gray eyes. He is tall and lanky, built like an endurance athlete. In fact, he is a long distance biker and regularly competes in the Labor Day bike-a-thon from Lansing to Upper Michigan. At work, he refuses to use the elevator and takes the five flight of stairs up and down for meeting between the offices.

"Hi Sanjeev," I start. "How did the bike-a-thon go last week".

"My wife joined me in the first leg. We took the scenic route. Finished second in my category," says Sanjeev breezily.

"Congrats Sanjeev", I say. "So how long was the ride?".

"It was 345 miles in total along the Lake Michigan shoreline," says Sanjeev with a self-assured grin.

"Wow," I say. I am impressed with his stamina, even in his early 50s. Sanjeev pulls up his laptop to discuss the platform issue.

Sanjeev is the VLE, the Vehicle Line Executive, responsible for the platform. He has a program manager like role, so his recommendations fall on functional managers like me for execution.

"Sanjeev, I saw your email and the numbers. Can you explain the Cost analysis?" I ask, trying to understand how the budget is put together for a new vehicle launch.

"Sure Steve. The vehicle budget is a big number. More than one billion dollars. It is made of two pieces – The capital budget, that covers plant upgrades and the revenue budget that covers expenses," says Sanjeev, explaining the background of new vehicle budgets. "In our case, vehicle testing & development, and plant & supplier tooling are expenses. Rest are capital upgrades."

"Sound simple enough" I say. "Can any of these expenses be avoided?" I continue.

"These expenses are critical for the new platform. In any case, we are a year after the first vehicle launch and they are spent money," he explains.

"Coming to the crux of the issue. The simple truth is that our dealers had to offer a higher sales incentive on passenger cars than we had planned," he continues. "If it continues, it will drive up the breakeven by 135,000 cars."

"How is the competition? Can we add any other variant model to compete with the competition?" I ask rather naively.

"You mean like expand the platform with a fifth vehicle?" asks Sanjeev. "That is a huge decision and has to be approved by the strategy board," he adds.

"No, no. Not that big in scope. How about adding more features to make our offerings more attractive? For instance, I see Subaru ads with in-car technology detecting sleepy drivers, that is being marketed to worried parents of teenagers," I ask.

"Yes, you got it. Subaru offers an enhanced safety package," says Sanjeev. "Hyundai offers a longer warranty and Honda has multiple cameras for collision detection."

"It will be another year before our features will leapfrog theirs," he adds. "But that is too late for the first two years of production".

"You said that a fifth vehicle is difficult to get approval. How is a vehicle package put together?" I ask. "It was fascinating for me, when I started in Supply Chain several years ago to learn that a unique exterior, you call a top hat, can define a unique vehicle"

"A unique top hat and the interior layout define the outside and inside looks for the vehicle," says Sanjeev. "But combined with 5 modules - the under body, the chassis, the interior structure, the electrical, and powertrain, they define the entire vehicle. We have these modules ready on shelf to combine whichever way to meet the marketing expectation where the car will sell," he continues.

"So, a top hat and the interior define the customer touch points for the vehicle. How long ago was the program approved?" I ask.

"These are 48 month programs. After a year of bubble up paper designs, the program goes to approval 36 months before production. Then it is time for cutting steel to make the first prototype," he says.

We spend the next two hours scrubbing the numbers. Starting from the pro forma profit statement for the CDX40, we end up with the expenses and income categorized into spending buckets.

- Engineering Design
- Testing expenses (design and production verification)

- Capital expenses -Plant tool up
- Supplier expenses
- Per piece cost at the plant
- Per piece cost at the supplier
- Marketing and sales
- Warranty costs

At the end it is very clear, that there are no easy savings opportunities.

"In my mind there are only two options to improve it. All other costs are already spent," I say finally. "One is the material cost reduction."

"How long do you expect is the payback period for material cost reduction?" he asks pensively.

"If we kick off now, I expect that the results will roll in a range from six months to two years," I say with a sigh.

"Why is that so long?" he asks curiously.

"The validation time for an approved change is a minimum 60 to 90 days. That is after the change is identified and approved," I tell him.

"And the second…" asks Sanjeev.

"Is warranty cost improvement. If the actual warranty can be reduced or the cost recovered from the suppliers," I say shifting focus.

"How quickly can this pay back?" he asks me. "I am not sure. But I expect that Chuck, our Supplier Quality Director, will have an answer as to how the current warranty situation is going. If there is a warranty cost due to supplier quality, we can capture that right away," I say confidently.

-The tale of two supply chains: Toyota and GM-

As Sanjeev gets up to leave, he says, "Supply Chain got us into this mess. I hope you can get us out of it".

"What do you mean, Supply Chain got us into this mess?" I ask taken completely by surprise.

"The starting point of this cost dilemma was the initial sourcing of suppliers. Our final supplier selection exceeded our cost target by 10 %" he says. "10 %".

"You know that it was our best cost during supplier negotiation," I say. "We did not have a good leverage, since we could not have a good volume projection, after our bankruptcy reorganization."

"You have to get us out of this mess," he says putting the focus back to supply chain.

"I will do my part. We have to work this together to see light at the end of the tunnel" I say knowing fully well that I need his help as much as he needs mine.

We decide to meet again later to discuss additional plans for the cost issue. We wrap up and Sanjeev hurries to another meeting.

After Sanjeev leaves, I have spent most of my morning reviewing the numbers.

Why are our car values so discounted? Our sales are affected by the resale value of the cars.

I remember Sanjeev's comment that about half of our sales are leases compared to the overall purchase of vehicles. That would mean that the cost of the car lease, will be dependent on the residual value of the car. Looking up the residual value awards for cars in Edmunds.com, I can see the difference in costs.

1. Average residual value of Honda SUV –65%
2. Average residual value of Toyota SUV – 63%

-The tale of two supply chains: Toyota and GM-

3. Average residual value of GM – 54%

So, I quickly send an email to JP Olenzek, the marketing VP to understand why the difference, especially what can be done from model year to model year.

While I was meeting with Sanjeev, Janet had come in and dropped off my updated phone. She has fixed my phone with IT help in two hours, that the AT&T rep could not fix at the store this weekend.

I send a quick text to Janet, asking her to get hold of Chuck for understanding the warranty situation. In a few short minutes, Janet has been able to touch base with Chuck, get him up to speed with the requirement, and sets up an appointment later in the day on my calendar.

The next few hours are tied up in a meeting with lawyers to document the details of a prior year program. There is a pending class action suit, so the documentation is accompanied by legal support. By the time I wrap up, I see that Chuck is waiting outside my office to meet me. I wave him in.

Chuck, our Supplier Quality director is an ex-marine, and prides himself on running a tight ship. As he walks into my office, I see that Chuck must be keeping up with his bootcamp routine of health and fitness.

"Good Afternoon Steve," starts Chuck in his husky voice.

"Good Afternoon. How are the kids doing these days?" I ask him.

"My eldest just enlisted in the marines," he says proudly. "And my daughter received the achievement award for the high school JROTC."

"Great to hear. I think that the kids are taking after their father well," I say.

-The tale of two supply chains: Toyota and GM-

"Tell me, why is the warranty expense high on the vehicle platform for this model year?" I ask switching subjects.

"Our quality metric at launch was not achieved this time. So, several ramp up issues turned into warranty cost," he says briskly.

"What is the recovery plan for quality? When will we reach the target quality?" I ask surprised.

"Our glide path to quality will reach target this month based on the current trend," he replies.

"That means that we have an excess cost of warranty. Have you diagnosed the root cause for these warranty issues?" I ask quizzically.

"We have analyzed the top 10 warranty issues so far. It is a mixed bag of supplier and plant issues," he says nonchalantly.

"When can you present those details to me," I ask feeling that this detail should have been escalated much earlier.

"I will ask Janet to block two hours tomorrow for the presentation," he says.

"I am offsite at the dealer council for the next two days. Please plan for Friday," I tell him. "I know that you are focused on the quality improvement. That is the right step. But, do you have a cost recovery plan for the issues?" I ask.

"I can present our cost planning to date as well," he says.

Chuck and I wrap up the conversation with the list of next to-do steps.

After Chuck leaves, I look at my watch, it is past 6pm. It has been a busy day.

On my way home, I think to myself. *Are there any opportunities for cost reduction to save the midsize car platform? How do the Japanese and the Koreans make money in this market?*

Chapter 5: Steve's plan
September 11, Friday
Global Motors HQ

I had been mulling over the mid-size platform and discussing with the dealer council for the past two days. I have not had a good night's sleep in the meantime. I am now convinced that we must get the suppliers to share our warranty cost as the first action in accountability and sharing the burden.

Chuck Rainer has a two-hour meeting slot scheduled with me this morning. Let's see what he has got laid out.

Chuck walks in exactly at 9am.

"Good Morning Steve," he says as he sets up his laptop and hooks his blue tooth connection to my computer monitor.

"G'Morning Chuck", I say. "How are you doing this morning?"

"Good, good" he says. "As you said yesterday, warranty is our biggest killer," he begins.

"We have analysed the top 10 warranty issues from the current launch. They are all connected with Engine or Powertrain warranty," he adds.

"Does product engineering agree that these are genuine warranty concerns?" I ask quizzically.

"That is an excellent question. About half the concerns are based on an NTF code," he says.

"NTF?", I ask not understanding the acronym.

"No trouble found. The supplier has analysed the returned parts and has not been able to reproduce the problem," he says.

"How is that possible for such a big percentage of parts?" I ask surprised.

-The tale of two supply chains: Toyota and GM-

"Say, a typical field return could be due to a vibration, when the customer engages the transmission on his truck," he says.

"So, when we test the returned unit transmission, it does not show a vibration problem, even though the dealer has replaced it under warranty to the customer!" I say incredulously.

"Yes. In some cases, the dealer has replaced the transmission two times at the same truck, and both returned units do not show a problem," he says further adding to my surprise.

Chuck opens a PowerPoint and explains the engineering behind why there could be a vibration in transmissions. While I like his preparation, I want to leave the technical solving to the Engineers.

"Should we not have the dealership talk to Engineering to see that the dealer is solving the right problem?" I ask.

"We are working with Engineering and the dealer to create a procedure for such cases," he says quickly anticipating my question.

"So, the dealer has no incentive to diagnose the right problem but does a swap out to keep the customer happy," I say summarizing the NTF issue. "And we compensate the dealer well."

"Maybe. But I take your point. I will talk to dealer relations team to get a process in place," he says finally.

"The dealer has to keep the customer happy, But I think that sometimes we have given the dealer too much liberty to make warranty decisions," I say.

"So, what about the other cases? Are these problems caused by the supplier or by our vehicle assembly plant?" I ask continuing the warranty discussion. "Do we have a plan to reduce warranty at our plant or at the least, at the supplier?"

"That part is still in the review stage," he says.

Chuck shows me another document that outlines a flowchart of how he is approaching the solution. I will leave that detail to Chuck and his team.

"I think we should review our warranty policy with the suppliers," I say conclusively. "Can you give me a breakdown of the costs?"

"Sure. I will send you a summary by email shortly," he confirms.

A few minutes after he leaves, I see his email summary.

From: Rainer, Chuck
Sent: September 11, 11:15 AM
To: Radue, Steven
Cc: Supplier Technical Managers
Subject: Warranty review summary

Good morning Steve:

Enclosed is the summary of warranty cost (in millions) for the prior year.

Total Warranty allocation (Budget): $250M

Engine: $80M

Transmission: $20M

Powertrain components: $60M

(Axles, 4x4, drivelines)

Other Vehicle Components: $20M

Total spent to date: $180M

I will investigate the dealer procedures with the appropriate teams and get back to you on or before September 15.

Thanks.

-Chuck

After my meeting with Chuck, I have a clear sense of how I should proceed. The first step is to get concurrence with George before making a policy change. So, I head over to George Anderson's office to make my case.

"Good morning George," I say as I knock and enter his office.

George is a big and tall man, in his late 50s. He is built like a line backer. I have a great deal of respect for him, since he started in the assembly line, got his degree and came up through the ranks. He is very perceptive and knows the company structure inside out.

"George, your presentation yesterday was very insightful. However, a bit alarming," I say.

"That was the intent," he says with a slight smile.

"Sanjeev and I have been discussing the Cost analysis and the options to move the business plan from red to black," I say getting right into the subject. "I spoke with Chuck as well. I see only two viable options. The material cost option and a warranty recovery plan."

"What changes do you propose?" he asks inquiringly.

"First in the warranty plan. I want to recover from the suppliers on their warranty expenses," I say seriously.

"How would you execute it?" he asks.

"Currently, we have an incentive-based warranty plan, where the supplier is rewarded for reaching or exceeding a warranty target. I want to recover all warranty from the supplier, and eliminate this incentive", I say.

"That is a bold step. Will it not damage our supplier relationship?" he asks questioning me.

"That is a risk that we may have to take," I say conclusively.

"Secondly, the material cost is based on our sourcing plan that picks up the best cost supplier. I want to change that to source the lowest cost supplier," I say.

"A best cost supplier has to meet our quality score. What if the lowest cost supplier does not have the right quality?", he asks perplexed.

"It will be up to Chuck and his team of Supplier quality engineers to work out the quality level at the supplier," I say.

There is a brief pause. "So, you expect Chuck to improve the supplier's quality after we award the business. That is a risky move," he says finally. "But will it get our program back in black?" he continues.

"Yes, we will reach half-way in the current project, but will reach full breakeven when sourcing reaches the right material cost at the next project," I say summarizing my conclusions from the last two days of review.

"I know that these are tough choices. But we need to reach back into full profitability in the business," he says nodding his head. "So, it is your prerogative. Go ahead with your plan."

When I return to the office, I put an email to the sourcing team to kick-off this new initiative.

From: Radue, Steven
Sent: September 11, 11:58 AM
To: Sourcing Board, Executive Sourcing Forum
Cc: Anderson, George; Kumar, Sanjeev
Subject: Warranty recovery plan

-The tale of two supply chains: Toyota and GM-

Good morning Team:

Based on Mr. Sanjeev Kumar's review of the midsize platform, it is clear that our platform costs are not under control. Since one key element of the cost basis, is the warranty allocation, I want to revise the warranty language on the future contracts, from an incentive-based plan to a straight cost recovery plan from the suppliers.

Please propose a new language for the contracts, so that we can standardize our contracts. I expect your proposal for this language by close of business on September 15.

Thanks.

-Steven Radue

VP, Supply Chain

I finish my lunch and head back to the office. As I walk into the office, I pick up the call from JP Olenzek. "Hey, Steve. Are you at your office?" he asks.

"Yes?" I reply.

"I read your email. I want to discuss used car values with you," he says briskly.

"I am headed to the townhall meeting. I can stop at your office on the way," I say.

A few minutes later, JP and I are sitting down in his office in front of his computer.

"One of thing that hurts our brand the most, as you know, is the residual value of used cars. About half of our customers are either lease buyers that keep the car for three years or less. Only about 18% of our customers keep the car till its end of life," he says. "We want to expand our sales to the folks that keep a car for life and for those that keep longer than a lease period."

He pulls us the website of cars with the best resale value. There are Hondas and Toyotas, but none of our cars.

"I am surprised that our cars are not on the list" I say.

"The resale value of larger SUVs and trucks are dominated by our products. But cars, car based SUVs and small trucks are not on the list," he says explaining the difference.

"How do we change that?" I ask.

"I am working with Engineering and warranty to improve the consistency of reliability on our vehicles," he says giving a focus to his resale costs. "We expect that we will have 20% more newer vehicles on the list next year. Our initial quality has exceeded our threshold."

"So, what can I do to help the quality image?" I ask him, trying to understand his direction.

"I know that you are rolling out the new warranty reduction and sourcing plan. We need to include the Supplier quality team to ensure that the supplier quality is improving, not reducing", he says emphatically.

"I agree with that 100%" I say with a smile, glad to have marketing support in our sourcing initiative.

"And I need our marketing plan to work with the dealers to ensure that our dealers address customer warranty problems through troubleshooting, and not by parts swapping," I add.

"I have heard that before. Please send me the exact cases that it has happened. I will address them," he says.

"I will ask Chuck to send them to you. But we need an overall procedure at the dealership location, so that we are not caught again in this conundrum," I say.

"I can't promise anything now. But if there is a systemic issue, I will address it," he says finally.

We wrap up our conversation and I am headed to the townhall meeting.

There are about 200 purchasing personnel at the auditorium for the town hall meeting. I want to bring up the two issues to the team.

We start the meeting with recognition of buyers who have 20 years of experience. The Purchasing director then accepts the State of Michigan Supply chain diversity award signifying that we have reached our goal of sourcing 10% threshold value to women owned business. Then it is my turn to address the team.

"What a great level of talent in this room. The team has performed very well. My role, as I see it is to set the guiding philosophy for the team. Every time we have established a goal, such as this diversity initiative, the team has exceeded it. Great work team," I say commending the team.

"So today, I want to institute two new requirements. Many of you know that our midsize platform is not making money. First is in sourcing. I want the sourcing teams to consider the low cost supplier, even if he has a low quality score." I say introducing the new sourcing guidelines.

"How will we close the loop. How do we get approval for that sourcing?" asks a buyer.

"You have to reach out to the Supplier Quality Engineering team," I say, pointing to Chuck. "If Chuck's team accepts the supplier, they will work with the supplier to raise the quality level at the supplier."

"The second action is the change in the warranty recovery plan. I have requested your Sourcing leaders to discuss and get back to me if we can implement a strict supplier repayment process for warranty," I add.

"When do you expect this change to be rolled out?" asks another buyer.

"I expect that we will bring this in the next 4 to 6 weeks," I say.

The town hall ends with a full Q&A session.

It is 4pm, when we are done with the meeting.

As I get back to the office, I pick up the phone to call Kevin. He had left me a volcemail earlier, about our trip tomorrow to visit our alma mater. I am looking forward to catch up with old friends and to meet the new football coach.

-The tale of two supply chains: Toyota and GM-

Supply Chain Management

Chapter 6: Kevin and Steve meet Neil
September 12, Saturday
Ross-Ade football stadium, Purdue University

It is just past noon, when Steve and I reach West Lafayette, Indiana, home of Purdue University. I see tailgaters in and around town, barbequing and lounging around before the game. Today Purdue plays Ohio State. Steve and I make the drive atleast twice a year to Purdue to watch the game and catch up with old friends.

We had a quick lunch on the way here to save time. We head straight to the stadium to get to our seats. Watching the game is a tradition between us, since Steve and I played for the college several years ago. Steve was a linebacker, when Drew Brees was the quarter back at Purdue. I was a wide reciever three years after Steve. We enjoyed college ball, but did not turn pro.

The stadium is fast filling up. Ohio State has a good team this year, but it is good to see Purdue in action.

The game is very close. In the first two quarters the lead goes back and forth between the teams. At halftime, the teams are still tied. *Is Purdue going to be a spoiler for Ohio State's chances at the Big 10 championship?* Purdue team is not ranked but plays well when they click and wind up with many upsets against ranked teams.

Steve and I make it to the concession stands at half time, when Steve spots Neil Armstrong ahead of us in the line. He is wearing a hat, possibly to avoid being spotted in the crowd, but Steve has a sharp eye. Picking up the beer and burgers, we catch up with Neil.

-The tale of two supply chains: Toyota and GM-

"Hello Neil, I don't know if you remember me," starts Steve. "but I was in the Senior class several years ago, when you brought the moon rock to Purdue".

"Steve, you are Kevin's brother," says Neil, to the our complete surprise. Neil recognized me, an Arts Major with a one time interaction with Neil, while Steve was in Neil's class.

"Hello Neil," I jump in to the conversation, walking behind Steve and Neil. Apparently, I must have made a big impression, when I joined the round-up quartet from the marching band and gave Neil a wakeup call at the hotel on his birthday, so many years ago. We spent the next 15 minutes recounting how I showed up with the band outside his window. Our band director was a good friend of Neil's and wanted to surprise him with a birthday serenade.

We have a lot of catching up in the next few minutes, but now it was time for the second half game to start up. Looking that Neil is there at the game by himself, Steve invites Neil to dinner. We typically join the Purdue football coaching staff at our favourite watering hole, the 9 Irish brothers. I am very surprised when Neil accepts, and Steve and I agree to pick him up at 6pm at his hotel.

The game ends at 4pm. Ohio State blew out Purdue in the second half, 41-20. We head to the hotel to checkin and freshen up.

I meet Steve at the lobby and we are ready to head out to pickup Neil. Steve updates me on our other friends that were planning to join us. The coaches, Jeff and Jeremy are delayed due to a last minute emergency among the players. They will try to join us, if they can get done.

We pickup Neil and head over to the restaurant. The restaurant is busy as it always is on a Saturday night. There is a live band playing Irish pub music. The hostess seats us at the

-The tale of two supply chains: Toyota and GM-

farthest corner, so that we can enjoy the music and maintain a conversation.

I order a rib eye steak, while Neil chooses today's special fresh tilapia and Steve orders a pepper steak.

"How did you decide on going to school at Purdue?" asks Neil.

"Kevin and I grew up in a small town near Fort Wayne," says Steve. "Our hometown is about 90 minutes from here. In my high school senior year, I visited Purdue, Indiana and Indiana State. Purdue offered me a football scholarship."

Neil looks at me, prompting the same question.

"I started at a community college. And then transferred into Purdue. I was a walk-on in the football program for the first year but got a scholarship the last two years of play," I continue.

I look around and I think to myself, *I am enjoying this dinner and conversation immensely. It is once in a lifetime that you would expect to catch up face to face with a real life hero on a personal level.*

"How about you?" I ask. "Purdue is known as a good astronaut school. But I expect that Neil when you joined, the astronaut program must have just started?" wondering how developed the University was in the 1950s when Neil was in school.

"I could have just well flipped a coin," says Neil breezily. "As you may know, I am from a small town in Ohio. In my high school senior year, I went to an Ohio State football game. Ohio State was playing Purdue. Not knowing much about the schools, I decided that I will choose my school based on the winner of that game."

I can't help but chuckle at Neil's reasoning and easy-going demeanor.

-The tale of two supply chains: Toyota and GM-

"How did you make it to the space program?" asks Steve curious that NASA came together in the 1960s, much after Neil's college graduation.

"I was and am passionate about flying. In fact, I got my pilot's license long before I got my driver's license," he says proudly. "I got into the air force after school and joined the war."

"Then President Kennedy gave America the challenge to go to the moon in the early 1960s. That galvanized the efforts. I was a test pilot for the early superfast flight programs and got recruited into the space program," he says in a very matter of fact voice.

The conversation winds into Steve's air force ROTC career and his move into the automotive working world.

"I know that the automotive industry is at tough cross-roads right now," says Neil. "I see the Detroit's Big three are in trouble in cost management, and the Japanese are struggling with quality during product launch."

Suddenly Neil gets my full attention.

"So, you must be following the news closely," I say.

"It looks like the companies are not learning from their own past lessons," says Neil. "Companies have their brand strength. But they are not capitalizing on their Supply Chain. In fact, they are working at cross purposes, using the supply chain as a means to an end, rather than as a strategic piece" he continues.

"What do you mean?" asks Steve. I can see from his face that his wheels are turning. *He must have struck a chord,* I think to myself.

"Product design is complicated. But in the automotive world, 80% of the product is driven by what the supply base can deliver.

-The tale of two supply chains: Toyota and GM-

So, if you look at this from a bottom up perspective, the Supply Chain is not tuned," says Neil.

Neil pulls out a napkin and draws a triangle and two boxes. "let's call this a Supply Chain framework for companies such as yours," says Neil.

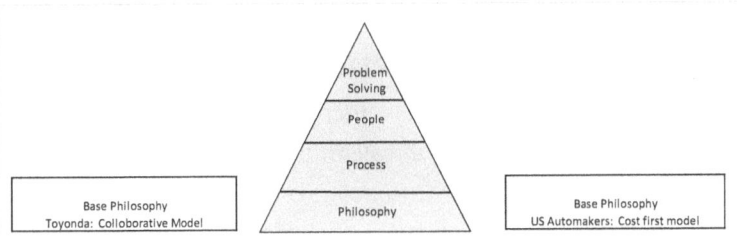

"Global motors competes on fresh design and low cost. So, any cost, especially cost of late changes are a killer. Toyonda competes on quality process in collaboration with the supplier. However, the American translation of these Japanese processes is slow," Neil continues.

I recognize the Supply Chain framework, from Jeffrey Liker's book, the Toyota way. But I am surprised by Neil's observation that all companies have the same framework. In addition, he believes that the companies differentiate each other by the strategy, not on the framework.

"How do smaller companies, such as Tesla create value?" asks Steve trying to understand the supply chain breakeven with small volumes.

"Tesla is adept at hyper-manufacturing, lean-agile supply chains and onsite additive manufacturing," says Neil to explain how small volume require a different manufacturing strategy. "Hyper manufacturing relies on smart giga factories."

"So that the plant can coordinate and change the manufacturing process smartly and quickly," says Steve, as he understands the breadth of the change. "Lean-agile supply

-The tale of two supply chains: Toyota and GM-

chain is the same for quick change ability of the supply base," I add.

"Yes. And additive manufacturing is where the parts are created at the point of use. Much like the food replicator on the Star Trek," says Neil with a smile.

"Is that even possible?" I ask, surprised that such a technology like the Star trek food replicator is available today.

"Yes, many parts especially custom plastic parts in low volumes, are made in such a way today. They are made from flowing plastic material that are cured in their final shape. Some steel parts for the aircraft industry is made the same way too," confirms Steve.

"I did not know your expertise in Supply Chain," says Steve finally looking at Neil. "I would like to discuss more one-on-one with you. Neil, can you spare me some time."

"Sure," says Neil. "I can see that Kevin and you are work competitors. So, I can plan on separate personal time, if Kevin, you are also interested."

Wow, I am amazed that Neil is able to vocalize what I have been thinking.

"Is there a conflict of interest with working with two companies?" I ask.

"The problem solving task is not a conflict. In the bigger picture, your product strategy is your product strategy. Supply Chain problem solving is executing to your goal," he says confidently.

A text message interrupts our conversation. "Delayed with a concussion protocol." It is from Jeff, and he can't join us for dinner. Neil looks up and asks Steve how concussion procedures have evolved since his game days.

"In my high school days, the coaches used to sit us out for a play or two, after concussion. Now-a-days concussion is taken more seriously," he starts.

"What is the current protocol?" asks Neil.

"There are five stages for the protocol, starting with step 1, a symptom limited activity," says Steve. "The final step is full football activity, after being cleared by a healthcare professional."

"I thought that NFL had such a protocol and not the schools," I chime in.

"NCAA lets the schools decide their own protocol and most schools follow the NFL style protocol," adds Steve. "In fact, I have some migraines from now and again, and am paying for my sins from long ago," says Steve.

I am completely surprised by Steve's admission, but Steve turns to me and says, "The doctors have cleared me, and there is nothing to worry about."

After dinner, the restaurant owner, Kurt walks to our table with a selection of delicious desserts. I choose a Tiramisu, while Steve loves his red velvet cake. Neil settles for some banana pudding.

The topic turns to aircraft building. Neil is involved in a project for building a world war II replica plane in his flying club in Ohio. He turns to Steve for advice. "The old engine that I have is not generating enough power in high altitudes. You have some experience in engines in the Air national guard. Will the newer engines be better replacement for the old ones?"

"I was a helicopter mechanic in the Air National Guard," says Steve. "The old engines had mechanical spark advance that was not quick enough for high altitudes."

"I have an experimental engine at my office labs. It has automatic electronic spark advance that is much quicker than the

-The tale of two supply chains: Toyota and GM-

old engine technologies," he says opening up some ways to collaborate with Neil.

"I would love to see the engine tests," says Neil.

"I will do one better. I can talk to the Engineering Director to see, if I can get you one of the new engines for your plane rebuild project," says Steve with a smile.

"That would be excellent," says Neil.

"I will let you know on Monday," confirms Steve.

Neil looks at my watch. "You have a dual zone Charles-Hubert watch. I take it that it helps you keep up with your design HQ on other time zones," he quizzes me gently.

"It is a gift from my wife," I say. "Sure, it helps to setup meetings in two time zones," I add, as Steve reaches out to pick up the check for dinner.

After dinner, we exchange contact information to continue the conversation later-on. As we drive and drop off Neil at his hotel, he says, "Remember, supply chain is about the right fundamentals, followed by strategy and practice."

"In fact, my mentor, Günter at NASA, used to say 'Übung macht den meister'."

"It means, Practice creates the Master, or loosely in English, practice creates progress and progress makes perfect."

On the drive back to our hotel, Steve and I are extremely quiet.

How is it possible for Neil to know the nature of the automotive business? His uncanny ability must be his qualification to lead the Apollo team. I need to tap his talent in solving my supply chain issues.

As we reach the hotel, the lobby is quiet. Steve convinces the night manager to reopen the bar and get us a late night shot of bailey's cream with whisky. After the shot, I head out to my room to call Donna, while Steve lingers in the lobby with his phone calls.

-The tale of two supply chains: Toyota and GM-

Supply Chain Management

-The tale of two supply chains: Toyota and GM-

Chapter 7: Balancing logistics with JIT
September 14, Monday
Toyonda Vehicle Assembly, Mississippi

Today I am back at the plant in Mississippi, for a meeting with the logistics team.

Last weekend, Steve and I had returned home on Sunday morning after visiting Purdue. Throughout the ride back we talked about the football game, but not much about Neil. As I dropped off Steve, he thought we should make a trip to visit Neil at his glider flight club in Ohio one of these weekends. Sure, that would be fun, I had told him.

My first meeting this morning is Rob Gonzalez, the logistics coordinator. If the supplier localization strategy has to work, then the JIT logistics has to work.

The overtime situation in the plant here, had subsided with our quality corrections at each supplier. However, Keith had made an accurate observation that the process was not robust to ensure that the situation does not repeat again.

Rob and I discuss the logistics problem. Rob explains the current logistics plan.

"Today, the plant uses 3 different logistics methods to manage incoming material," he explains. "I am responsible for two of these three methods with our trucks. One is the local pickup & delivery, we call milk runs. Our milk run trucks pickup supplier parts within a 200 mile radius, with most suppliers being within the first fifty. The second method is for overseas parts, that we pick up from the shipping port."

"What is the third method and who manages that?" I enquire.

"Third method is supplier FOB destination. That just means that the supplier delivers the parts to the plant in the JIT sequence and in the JIT timing. Here I coordinate the incoming schedule, but use the supplier's trucks in the process," he adds.

"Parts from the port are long lead time parts and have been steady incoming. There is not much churn and so managing these are not difficult", he continues. "However, with the milk run, we are running at 95% truck usage with about 62% load capacity," he says pointing to his tracking metric on the wall.

"So, your trucks are moving a lot, but only at about two thirds full," I say surprised while looking at the wall graphs.

"And one of our longest pickups is from a new supplier in Arkansas. The truck runs 8 hours every day at an average of just over half full," he adds.

"So, you have one or two trucks dedicated to this supplier, just to have a constant flow of parts every day?" I say surprised that we have such a situation.

"With 6 new suppliers added this year, and 20 coming up shortly, the flow of parts is not optimized. So, there is a lot of wastage of trips," confirms Rob.

We spend the next hour looking through the possible route combinations for all the current suppliers and the proposed new suppliers.

"You need to double your truck fleet," I say finally looking at the total load that he must carry at the end of the day.

That is a major change in logistics philosophy. That won't work, I think to myself.

"You know Rob, the company will not go for that", I say with a sigh. "Suppliers may have to commit to their own delivery plan."

"Let me discuss this with the Japan logistics team," I finally tell him, seeing no easy solutions. "They may have to simulate this variation in software to see if the best routes and timing requirements can be met. There may better options to go forward."

"The other item that I wanted to discuss with you, was the incoming sequencing. Were there any issues in the JIT deliveries this month that contributed to the overtime issue in the plant?" I ask curious if the tight 90 plus percentage utilization of transportation now, resulted in exceeding capacity this month.

"Good question. I have some facts and figures that I want to discuss on that issue," he says.

"We had 8 containers expedited this month. That is 16 hours of overtime," he continues to my surprise.

"So is this still part of the plant overtime tracking. Is it not?" I ask naively. "Yes, yes. But the overtime compounds when we have to open containers out of sequence," he says brashly.

"In short, you are saying that since you are running at 95% usage level, your efficiency suffers when the plant expedites material and you have to scramble over your transportation capacity," I summarize his statement.

"True, true" he says, when we have the plant delivery manager walk in asking Rob to help with a belligerent driver.

"I think that I have all I need for now. I will check back with you if I need additional details," I say as I am walking out through the door.

As I walk out, I see that the receiving dock is right behind Rob's office. I can see one of the drivers is in a heated discussion with Rob. The plant has a zero tolerance policy for drivers abusing alcohol and it looks one of the drivers has alcohol under his breath. The driver is upset stating that he had some Nyquil, not alcohol after the truck was delivered. Rob is calmly advising him that he should talk to his contract house for the next steps. Today, his truck will not pick up the return load until an alternate driver is located.

-The tale of two supply chains: Toyota and GM-

As I walk back to my desk, I think about how different my work experience is from school. I remember the Supply Chain professor discussing economic order quantity, or EOQ in every transaction. We have delivery quantities that are now in daily usage levels and not EOQs. The overseas shipments come in 4 to 6 week bundles. And the just in time logistics is delivered at 4 hour usage bundles. How different is the working reality than from a textbook? And the plant makes the body panels and other internal parts that come in continuous flow, just like JIT.

I head to Jorge's office to discuss his findings from the quality and overtime issues earlier this month. Jorge is wrapping up his meeting and motions me to sit down.

"Kevin," says Jorge, putting down the phone. "Jorge" I respond taking a seat.

"I hear that three of the six issues were supplier quality issues and have permanent corrective actions for solving the issue," I say. "However, I am waiting to discuss with the supplier development team, to understand that the permanent fix has the right metrics behind it. So that we can track to ensure that it does not repeat."

"Please include me when you discuss the metrics with David," he says. "Meanwhile, the other three problems were mistaken logistics"

"Or JIT failures, two at the plant and one at the supplier" I state the obvious.

"No way," starts Jorge defensively.

The plant tracks and receives more than 100 containers of material every-day. The logistics team unpacks these containers in the right sequence so that the line can be fed with the right parts.

"We have been doing this from day one, when the plant started production. You say that this month we had a few

-The tale of two supply chains: Toyota and GM-

containers unpacked wrong," he says with his typical deadpan expression.

"I understand your surprise. However, if some parts are to be expedited, then the sequence should accommodate the changes to get the right parts for the build on time." I start to explain the logic behind the error.

"I just spent the last two hours with Rob in logistics. He has traced the error to 8 containers that were unpacked wrong due to the expediting rush, that caught his team off guard," I continue.

"If more than a few containers are expedited, then the plant has to do a manual tracking to get the right sequence. Everything can go awry," I add.

Jorge has a look of disbelief about him and is not buying my explanation. "You should discuss this with Rob as well," I say to get him a second opinion.

"Well, there is another problem brewing in logistics," I continue. "He is asking for more trucks to meet the scheduling needs".

"You know that I can't justify more trucks," Jorge summarizes.

"I know that the logistics efficiency is poor. Let me bring in the Japan logistics simulation team to discuss how to solve it," I continue.

"How long will it take before we can look at possible solutions?" asks Jorge.

"I expect that we can discuss some details in two days," I say briskly. "I believe that the late changes to the build sequence is the root cause."

"Do you have any proof?" he asks.

"No numbers to prove yet. But I suggest we freeze the build sequence earlier, so that we can minimize the expediting every time. Less expediting gives less chance for a risk" I tell him.

"I can't make such a big change now. This kind of change requires the board level approval and has to be presented at the annual review," says Jorge.

"Can you implement a temporary freeze of the build sequence, six weeks ahead of the build," I ask him.

"Six weeks is impossible," he says.

We discuss the ramifications of such a change and the approvals that we need. Jorge finally agrees to work on a two week pull ahead to create a four weeks frozen schedule.

"I will work with the Plant manager to get his approval. I suspect that the Sales department would have to signoff since they have less ability to affect late changes," he says.

As I am walking to my office, the phone rings.

"G'Afternoon, Kevin here", I answer the phone on the second ring.

"Hello Kevin" says Lynn. I did not expect a call from her. "Bill would like to see you. When can you come here?"

The last meeting with Bill is still etched in my mind. While we have addressed the day to day issues from the new supplier quality concerns, we are still way behind on creating the systems for ensuring smooth operation for these concerns.

I knock and enter Bill's office. Keith is sitting there with Bill. "Good Afternoon, Bill. Good Afternoon, Keith", I say.

"G' Afternoon," each of them say to me.

"I have been discussing with Keith about our quality issues. He believes that you have done an excellent job in reaching out to the suppliers and our plant teams," says Bill.

"You know that Keith is leaving back to Japan this month. I want to appoint you as the new Regional Supply Chain manager," says Bill.

I am pleasantly surprised. I have been working hard on Bill's task and have completed the corrective action. But I am not close to the point of dealing with the process root causes and Keith knows this. *He must know that I am on the right track.*

"I wanted to let you know that in person, and be the first to congratulate you," says Bill. Keith smiles and nods in agreement.

I am dumbfounded and I can just mutter the words, "Thank you. I appreciate your confidence in me. However, I would like to take a day or so, talk it out with my family before I can move forward."

"I know that Keith has some points that he wants to discuss with you. So, I let you two to continue the conversation," says Bill.

As Keith and I walk out of Bill's office towards the conference room, Keith congratulates me on the job.

Keith was my first boss, when I started from school and he has always been my mentor.

Keith starts the conversation as we sit down in Bill's private conference room. "The short-term solutions for the quality issues are starting to fall together. What is the long term direction?" He starts right where he left off, during our last conversation at his Michigan office.

I start with the cultural issues of the Toyonda Supply Chain philosophy. I tell him about Neil and his insights into the translation of Toyonda's process plans through the culture. Keith listens intensely and how multiple companies use the same structure, and get different results based on the Supply Chain base philosophy.

-The tale of two supply chains: Toyota and GM-

"It looks like to are getting to the crux of the issue," he says finally. "Remember, if you don't solve the root cause, fixing the symptoms will only get you through that day. We will fail miserably at the next symptom of the same root cause."

Keith and I review the supplier list and discuss how the Supply Chain implementations can be tuned to meet the American supply base.

Keith wraps up the conversation, as he gets ready to head to the airport for his flight back to Michigan.

Finally, I have some time to call Donna. I reach her, while she is visiting the neighbors.

"Hey Honey. How is your day going?", I start.

"Hey. I was expecting your call later today. Is everything going OK?" she asks in a worried voice.

"Yes Donna. Are you busy with the neighbors? Can we talk for a few minutes?" I ask in a bubbly voice.

"Sure, what's up?"

"I want to give you the good news, Donna. Bill called me to his office and gave me the Regional Supply Chain Manager position," I tell her, hardly holding back my gush at becoming the youngest manager in that executive role.

She is excited and wishes me well. We plan on a family celebration dinner, when we can tell the kids.

I wrap up the call with some additional notes and promise to call her when I reach the hotel.

It is 6pm, by the time I check in to the hotel. Overall, it has been a good day personally. Now that the promotion buzz has settled in, I realize that I need to go a longways to solve the Supply Chain problems.

I freshen up and spend the next half hour on Skype Video with Donna and the kids catching up on their daily routine. I head to the hotel restaurant to watch the Monday night football and grab some dinner.

Just then, I have an email notification from the legal department. I had earlier sent them a note to confirm the details on if I can retain Neil as a consultant. I was not sure, if there would be a conflict of interest, since Neil is talking to Steve and me. But apparently most supplier consultants are in similar situation and manage that balance. *That is a green light.*

I look up my calendar agenda for tomorrow. David had requested a timeslot to discuss his findings on supplier culture. *How can we get new suppliers into the Ecosystem culture? A culture change? I wonder what he is proposing.*

-The tale of two supply chains: Toyota and GM-

Supply Chain Management

Chapter 8: When lean meets constraints
September 15, Tuesday
Toyonda Plant, Mississippi

I head to the plant early in the morning for a call with the Japanese logistics planning team. As I step into the conference room, I see that David has sent me the meeting request for 11am. David Joseph is the Supplier Development Shukko.

The meeting is about kaizen report out on supplier readiness for implementing lean processes. It is a long winded subject title for the meeting request. But lean is core philosophy of supply chain, so supplier readiness to embrace leanness is crucial for success. I remember his earlier conversation, where he had found some of the new suppliers not wanting to implement lean practices.

David's meeting request has a meme, next to the request. I chuckle at the picture and wonder what David has in store for me at the meeting.

Can you teach an old dog?

Rob is already in the conference room. Takao and Shintaro join us from Japan. They have reviewed our information and have done some simulation. This is quick, a one-day turnaround, I think to myself.

"Kon'nichiwa Takao San and Shintaro San," I start the conversation.

I hear "Kon'nichiwa" echo from each person. Then Takoa takes the lead to explain what they have done so far.

"I am not sure if you are aware of the simulation process," says Takao. "There are several variables such as the planned build schedule and any last minute variations to such a plan. We start with the supplier's relative location from the plant," he continues.

"A single successful simulation is when the trucks can get the material from all the suppliers to the plant for the next day production," he adds.

"The results are valid, when we can run hundreds of variations for each strategy that we choose," concedes Shintaro.

"How many strategies have you tried so far?" I ask.

"We have tried three strategies so far," says Takao.

The Japanese team then posts a slide of the results.

First pass results
(Baseline capacity utilization at 62%)

S.No	Strategy	Projected results
1	Supplier drop off from one Arkansas supplier and One tenessee supplier	Reduce by one truck. Capacity utilization 75%
2	Pickup of Western suppliers on Monday, Wednesday and Friday. Northern suppliers on Tuesday and Thursday and Eastern suppliers on Monday and Thursday.	Capacity increase from 62% to 68%
3	Redesign routing with cross docking facilities	Additional cross dock needs to be budgeted. Simulation pending.

"I see that the team has done a lot of work, in a very short duration" I say impressed that they had less than 24 hours since I wrote them my email note yesterday.

"I am not sure that these strategies are realistic so far. However, I like the cross-docking facility option. Can the team look at specific locations for cross docking and run some additional simulations?" I ask.

"Sure. I think that was our next step anyways," says Takao positively.

"How long will you need to run these simulations in more detail?" I continue.

"Maybe another 48 hours" says Takao.

"Let's plan a follow up meeting on Friday," I say hoping that we can have a more detailed and substantive discussion.

Takao agrees to setup the follow-up meeting and we wrap up our conversation.

I realize that I am late to my next meeting and rush up to meet David and Jorge.

David and Jorge are already at the conference room when I walk in. David has the picture of the bulldog on the screen.

"What's up with the roller skating bulldog?" asks Jorge.

"I know that you are a Georgia football fan. So, can you teach your team mascot to roller skate?" I tease David, since he is a University of Georgia Alum and an ardent football fan.

"I was setting up the context for today's review of new supplier audits," says David. "Many of our suppliers have supplied to the local auto industry for several years. They process all their current production in batches. This goes against our lean philosophy of an assembly line, where all parts are processed as one piece flow – one at a time through the line," he says.

I was not expecting this bombshell. Our purchase agreements clearly state that all suppliers will follow lean processes. Lean process is based on low in process inventory and one piece flow.

"How do they ensure they meet the production schedule?" asks Jorge.

"They follow the theory of constraints," says David.

"What is this theory?" I ask.

"In simple terms, the theory of constraints is about managing the factory around a bottleneck resource. Production is scheduled around ensuring that the bottleneck resource is not being starved of parts," says David.

"That sounds like batch production. Our prior director, Tachi Ohno established that our industrial success is based on single piece process and eliminating waste. I thought that these were the fundamentals of lean and of Supply Chain. In fact, our purchase agreement explicitly states the supplier should follow lean process" I repeat my concern and confront the gap in supplier commitment.

"Is the supplier violating the contract by ignoring lean concepts?" asks Jorge.

"Maybe," says David. "But can we teach them to follow lean?"

"It sounds like the supplier is saying no" says Jorge.

'This is a good question for Neil," I say after a long pause.

I tell them about my meeting with Neil and my planned follow up call with him at 3pm today.

We agree that David should join me as we can discuss some of these concepts to pick Neil's thoughts.

It is 2:30pm. We head out to a late lunch at the cafeteria and continue the discussion.

At 3pm, David and I meet at the conference room for the call. I dial Neil's skype number and reach him at his office.

"Good afternoon Neil. Are you back at Ohio after the weekend?" I ask. Neil is teaching a class at Cincinnati today and has only a short time before he must head back to his office.

"Yes Kevin. How was your ride back?" he asks.

"Good Neil. I have David from Supplier quality with me. I also have some good news. I think we can get you on a consulting contract. Can you tell what rates would make sense for putting you on a contract?" I ask gently.

He tells me to pay him a tenth of what I save from his ideas. Neil is not firm on his expectation. I know he is not really concerned about the payment terms for such a contract. I promise to send him the contract document so that we can retain his services.

David and I then explain the dilemma with lean implementation at new suppliers.

"Suppliers are willing to produce by batch process, but not through the lean requirement of single flow," summarizes David.

"What do you think that you are losing by letting them follow a batch process?" he asks softly. David explains that lean would be the more efficient process. Neil stops him in the middle.

"I don't agree that lean is the most efficient," says Neil. "A lean journey is what you want from the supplier, not a static lean process."

He opens the computer sketchpad and draws a quick picture for us. He shows the picture on the screen.

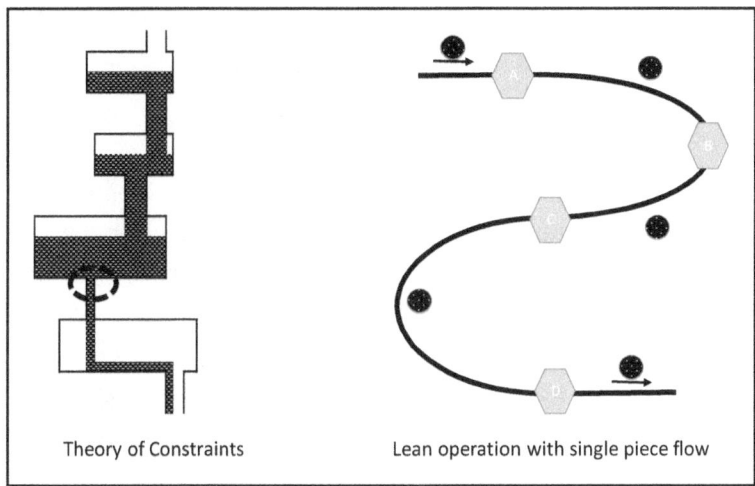

Theory of Constraints Versus Lean Flow

"Theory of constraints is like making water flow down a series of tanks. You must make sure that the narrowest orifice does not constrain the total output. Every assembly line has a bottleneck much like the narrowest orifice. The line output is dependent on how you manage this bottleneck. The slowest machine in the assembly line paces the output" says Neil diligently.

"Now, lean is about exposing this bottleneck constraint to the next operation, thus balancing the line, so that the line is moving forward at the right pace," he continues.

"So lean and theory of constraints can coexist," summarizes David.

"Exactly," says Neil. "Reducing the work in process inventory, is like draining the swamp. The rocks in the river are problems that cannot be eliminated until the water is low enough to expose them," he adds. Then Neil brings up another picture on the sketch pad.

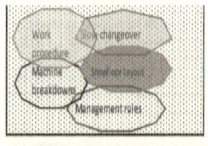 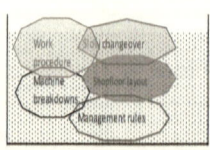 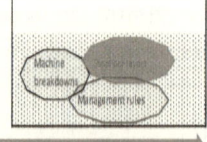

Lean Journey

"As long as we have a high level of in-process inventory, the issues that cause waste are not visible. In my experience, rigid work procedures and slow changeover process when the line changes from one product to another are the top level rocks. But in reality, any issue can lead to waste. The only way to find the waste is to drain" says Neil emphatically.

"After the first drain, we can eliminate the first level rocks. Then we must drain some more to expose the other rocks, such as the three rocks in your example," summarizes David.

"So, the lean journey is good. If the supplier can continue the journey, reducing the in-process inventory and eliminating the line delays," I confirm.

"Correcta mundo," says Neil.

"And this is one step in the cultural transformation, that you were suggesting for Toyonda", I add.

Neil and David agree. We wrap up the conversation with a few other observations and close the meeting.

Heading back to the airport, I am trying to catch a later flight than my usual trips back from Mississippi. But I feel good that we are making progress.

Wow. This is the first sign of progress and it feels good. Can we sustain it?

-The tale of two supply chains: Toyota and GM-

Supply Chain Management

-The tale of two supply chains: Toyota and GM-

Chapter 9: A Small supplier's guide to survival
September 16, Wednesday
Toyonda HQ, Michigan

It is Wednesday morning. I am back at the headquarters. The morning has been very busy with phone calls. Bill had sent out a broadcast message about my promotion and there were several calls of congratulations. *I have the job, but how come I still feel that I have a lot to learn on the job.*

At 9am, we gather in the auditorium for Keith's farewell. Bill is joined by a video link and addresses the audience. "During Keith's time in Supply Chain, our US sales has gone up from 4.5 million to 7 million vehicles and Supply Chain department has gone from under 100 personnel to 350 personnel. Thanks Keith, for a job well done. I know that we will continue to work with you in your role across the pacific."

"*Yoi tabi o.* Bon voyage," he congratulates Keith.

One by one several people address Keith and his accomplishments. Now it is my turn. "I remember the day, that Keith came to campus recruitment   I was not sure that I was a good fit for the company, since I was a business major. But Keith coached me all along the way to a career in Supply Chain. Thanks Keith, for being my boss and my coach."

After the farewell speeches, we are served some cake and snacks. Being close to lunch, I do not have much of any snacks. Later, I walk back to his desk and catch up with Keith. Keith is excited to hear the new cultural aspects of the Supply Chain philosophy. He has a smile of approval when I describe my conversation with Neil. We wrap up when the movers come to his office.

At 11am, my stuff is all moved into Keith's office. I hear a gentle knock on the door. Josh Herrera is here for his meeting.

The tale of two supply chains: Toyota and GM

He has requested some time to discuss some findings in the new supplier launch process.

Josh opens his computer and walks me through his presentation. Among the new suppliers on tap for the launch, and others under review for the next phase, he believes that a trend is emerging.

There are 9 small companies in the review. Each one of the small companies is struggling in the launch process.

"What is your yardstick for a small company?" I ask curious how he has identified the group.

"These companies are all small widget makers, from washers, nuts and bolts to tubes and wiring harnesses. They have a capitalization under $1 million and a turnover under $5 million," he explains.

"What areas are they struggling?" I ask trying to get a magnitude of the concern.

"In the launch category, we evaluate them on 13 areas, ranging from planning, process readiness, process validation to manufacturing feasibility. Each company is struggling in a different area," he says briskly.

"So, they are not investing in processes and cannot reap the benefits like larger companies. Is there a pattern in their struggle?" I ask.

"I have thought long and hard about this," he says. "I believe it is just that their experience base is rather limited."

"I know that most Auto companies would not care. But our guiding philosophy is that we are one supply base, us and our suppliers together. So, I see this as an opportunity to improve supplier relations," he says.

"Good point. How would our Japan plant handle it for their suppliers?"

"That's the rub," he says. "Our company has developed the ecosystem of suppliers in Japan. Suppliers share their solutions to common problem and large suppliers share their problem-solving process with smaller suppliers."

I have long heard of this process among Japanese suppliers. The famous story of how Aisin Seiki shut down production for Toyota in the late 1990s, and the resulting response is legendary. As the story goes, when Aisin's P-valve plant burnt down, Aisin shared its drawings with many of its suppliers to find an alternate source for Toyota production. About 10 companies responded with Denso successfully making duplicate parts in 60 days, while offloading its own parts to another secondary supplier to make room. All in all, demonstrating a loyal supply base.

"That is called the theory of collective mutualism," says Josh. "It is an unwritten rule in the ecosystem, that the Supply Chain itself works as a single entity. What is good for the customer, is good for the ecosystem."

"But loyalty works both ways. When the customer is first, both the Auto company and the supplier work for their mutual benefit," he continues.

"How does a supplier get compensated going above and beyond the requirement?" I ask.

"In the Denso case, Toyota paid two months of profits to Denso and others that helped them for their extra effort," he says.

How will this work? Is it reasonable to expect no self-interest? "That will not work here," I say vocalizing my thoughts. "We need to invent a process to share information."

"Meanwhile, please let me know if you need additional manpower to get the suppliers up to speed," I add thinking of other approaches that can help Josh to reach his goal.

I make a mental note that I should discuss this Ecosystem cultural issue with Neil.

"Small suppliers have some advantages too," I say. "I expect that many small suppliers will have a good cost structure. Even better than larger suppliers for smaller technology components. Isn't that right?" I ask Josh.

Josh agrees. "However, they are personnel dependent and may not be able to add new talent to bring in new processes," he confesses.

After a moment's pause, "True," I confirm.

"So how can we help these suppliers without incurring an additional cost for them during economic tight times," I ask.

"We need another system for training the supplier," says Josh energetically. "How is the training done in Japan?" he asks.

"At our parent company, we have a series of nested suppliers. The Tier 1 supplier has a controlling effect on the Tier 2s," I say confirming the Keiretsu arrangement in Japan.

That won't work here, we conclude after debating the plusses and minuses for such a strategy. "We need to invent an Auto company led tiered learning activity to create a quick learning process throughout the Supply Chain," I say finally.

"How will that look like?" asks Josh.

"I don't know yet. But we need to figure that out fast," I say.

"How about the financial stress for small companies in times such as during these pandemic outbreaks?" asks Josh.

"Good question," I say. "That needs a financial solution. Something that requires Bill's intervention."

"Let me put an email to him now," I add.

Josh and I pen an email to Bill to cover the financial distress concern.

From: Radue, Kevin
Sent: August 31, 1:35 PM
To: Zemanski, Bill
Cc: Herrera, Josh
Subject: Supplier financial strain

Hello Bill:

Josh and I have been reviewing the status of small suppliers during these pandemic times.

It is clear that about a quarter of the small suppliers have undergone a tough financial year. I know that without our intervention some of them will go under. Is there any financial assistance that we can offer them?

Regards
Kevin Radue

Josh is wrapping up to leave, when I see that Bill has responded back to us. In short, his email reads that the company would be ready to change the accounts payable terms from the current 90 days to 30, 45 or 60 days, depending upon the supplier's current situation. Any such change will be temporary, and would be phased out after 6 months, and should save the supplier substantial money to further strengthen their balance sheet.

"Wow, this is a major help," says Josh.

I agree with him that this will make the suppliers happy.

"Can you put a list of suppliers and their current situation. Let's take it back to Bill for his approval, supplier by supplier," I say.

Josh will get back to me by next Monday for our discussion with Bill.

By the time I look at my watch it is late, and I pick up the phone to call Donna to tell her that I am on the way home. One more step in the culture change.

I look up my upcoming calendar. There is a call with the Japanese team to discuss the solution for the logistics dilemma. *I wonder if the team has been able to work out the logistics to add the next batch of new local suppliers. I am eager to find out their solution proposals.*

Chapter 10: Minimizing variation
September 18, Friday
Kevin's home, Brighton, Michigan

I begin the day with a cup of coffee and a bagel, as I get started in the early morning call to Japan. 6am call is far too early to take this call at work. Donna has a neat office area at home with two 27" monitors for an extended view of the computer screen. She has agreed to let me use this space today for my meeting. Knowing that she is OCD on keeping the place organized, I will make sure that the place is back to the same condition when I leave.

I login to the WebEx conference with the Japanese Logistics team, Takao and Shintaro. Rob joins us, as we get started.

"Kon'nichiwa Takao San and Shintaro San," I start. "Good morning Rob."

"Kon'nichiwa," says Takao, Shintaro and Rob.

"How are you all doing today?" I add.

I hear "Doing well." After some catch up on the Japanese weather, we get started.

I address Takao on what he has discovered from his simulation results. Takao explains his process, "We have done over a thousand simulations of production sequencing with on-time and expedited deliveries from all the local suppliers."

He describes the details further. "The mechanics of the simulation requires random variation within the specified range and seeing the effect on the results. It is called Monte Carlo simulation, a standard process named after the casino simulation done many years ago in Monte Carlo."

"As you know that the current situation is not sustainable. We have two solutions. One is increasing the number of trucks by 50%"

The first solution will require a substantial higher investment. How is this feasible? I think to myself.

"The second option is to create two regional cross dock facilities," he continues.

With some quick math on outsourced cross dock facilities, we estimate that the cross-dock facility will cost 18% of the increased cost of additional trucks.

"Where would you recommend the cross docking?" I ask wondering if this solution can be viable.

"Our recommendation is that one facility be located between Memphis, Tennessee and Little Rock, Arkansas. The second should be located close to Birmingham, Alabama," says Takao.

Looking at the map, that's where most of the new suppliers are located.

"How wide a coverage will this give us? Can we reach all of our local pickups?" I ask getting excited that this solution could work. "Our coverage is 100%," he says.

"What is the expected peak load usage capacity with this plan?" I ask, knowing that this will be deciding factor. "We estimate that it will be 65% now, rising to 85% when you complete the next phase of the localization projects," chimes in Shintaro.

"This looks like it is great progress," I say finally. "Can you put a report together?" I continue. Takao agrees to send the report by next Monday. Rob and I schedule a time to put a presentation together, so that I can present to the board for cost approvals.

"Please include the simulation results for the options that did not work as well," I tell Takao, so that I have enough information to convince the board.

We wrap up the call after agreeing on how to proceed forward.

An hour later I am at my desk at work. I start with reviewing my calendar for the day. Just then, I see an email pop up in my inbox from Tom Nakamura, the Plant Manager. I open the email.

From: Nakamura, Tom
Sent: September 18, 11:20 AM
To: Radue, Kevin
Cc: Joseph, David; Edwards, Jonathan; Herrera, Josh
Subject: Supplier constraints at Plant #1

Hello Kevin:

This week, I had a call from two suppliers. Both suppliers are from our Supplier Council. They are concerned with not being able to keep up with the production requirements and variation. Please review with your team and give me your recommendations.

Thanks

-Tom Nakamura
Plant Manager
Mississippi Plant #1 and 2

I pick-up the phone and call Josh Herrera. "Josh, I got an email from Tom. You are in the cc for that email. Tom is asking about suppliers not keeping up with production variation," I ask.

Josh pulls up the email, while I am on the phone to get caught up.

"First of all, are you familiar with the issue. And secondly, is this connected to the small size supplier issue that we discussed earlier this week," I ask.

"No, not really," says Josh. "Let me join you in your office," he says.

Josh is there in a few minutes and we continue the conversation.

"You are aware of the freeze, thaw and slush rating for the production schedule," he starts. I know that the three different schedules are the period of how frozen the build schedule is during the build plan.

In the three-month production plan, called the "Slush", the schedule is laid out for the incoming material and what vehicles are assigned for sales to what dealers. However, the dealer has a one-month window to request changes in the vehicle assignment and options that are installed in the vehicle. These options can be backup cameras, collision avoidance controls, high end sound system, leather seating, vehicle and interior color etc. This period is called the "thaw".

In the current month, all schedules are frozen, hence the term "Freeze" and very few changes are possible. Only post manufacturing additions, such as dealer installed options are allowed.

"In the last three months, the company has reduced the freeze zone to align the production with the dealer's sales needs. Dealers are allowed changes until 21 days before the build. This means that the suppliers need to scramble their production line in a two to three-week window," he says.

"I thought that I had spoken to Jorge about this when we were dealing with the expedited delivery issue this week?" I say seeing that we are tackling the same issue from the production side.

"Jorge is working on some of the short-term changes. But we need a better visibility and a long-term perspective," he says.

"Interesting that production supply is requesting a firmer schedule, just like logistics was requesting last week," I say connecting the two dots together.

"The Corporate philosophy was better aggregate demand" says Josh.

"Something does not connect. I thought that aggregation of demand, had smoothed out the requirements," I say. Aggregation was the idea that when you combine the changes from several dealers, they average out. By balancing the additions to the subtractions, they lead to minimal changes in the build. The company had launched this concept just a few months ago.

Josh is thinking through a long pause. "I am not sure that aggregation is working," he says finally.

"Ok, we need to discuss this with Tom," I say. Reaching out to my phone, I dial Tom's number. Tom is not reachable. So, I schedule a meeting with him at 1pm through his secretary.

"Josh, please come back to my office at 1pm, for the call with Tom," I say.

After a quick lunch, Josh joins me at my office for a phone call to Tom.

"Hello Tom," I start the conversation.

"Hello Kevin. Congrats on the promotion," says Tom.

"Thanks Tom," I say. "I saw you email and wanted to connect with you. I have Josh in the room with me."

"Hello Josh," says Tom. "This is definitely up your alley".

"Yes Tom. I know that some of the suppliers are struggling with the changes to our freeze point," says Josh.

"Oh, oh. I thought that it was a supplier issue. Maybe it is a reaction time issue," says Tom.

"Regardless, we need to put in some limits to the freeze point changes," I say.

"What do you suggest?" asks Tom.

"On the short term, I believe that we should limit the changes at the supplier end, by say 10%," I say. "So, the supplier cannot see more than 10% change from the thaw to the freeze point."

"Another option is to create a gradual transition between the thaw and freeze zones," I add.

"You mean like another intermediate zone," says Tom. "I have the scheduling manager in the room & he is shaking his head no. Give me a minute, let me talk to him," he says, putting the phone on mute.

Coming back online, he adds, "The intermediate zone idea will not go well here."

"So, you are suggesting that either walk back the freeze zone to 4 weeks or install some controls to limit the variation in the 4th week," says Tom.

"We are also planning to limit the build model combinations to the high sellers," he says.

"What does that mean?" I ask.

"We will build 20% of the models that contribute to 80% of the sales," says Tom.

"Aha, the 80-20 rule," I say.

"Yes, kind of the pareto rule," says Tom. "We will also eliminate 5% of the models that sell less than 10 days-worth of production in a year."

"Have you thought about linking the customer bundles, such as Economy bundle, Deluxe or Luxury options with aggregated supplier forecast," I say.

"Are you saying that we can force the customers to pick from just three specifications of vehicles?" asks Tom incredulously. "If that will work for you," I add.

"I need to run that past marketing and the board, to make such a dramatic change," he says. Josh and I concur.

"If we are brainstorming ideas to reduce variation, here is another one. You can consolidate the base content such as wiper accessories and radio buttons to one color – say black," adds Josh.

"Overall, I am not convinced that aggregation is working," says Tom, bringing us back to the root cause of the supplier's concerns. I am happy to hear that Tom agrees with managing aggregation, echoing the sentiments that I heard from Josh earlier. I know that Jorge and I had several conversations about the freeze point and have not moved forward. I will have an easier time, if Tom, Jorge's boss is onboard with addressing the freeze point changes.

"I will talk to my consultant and get back to you on aggregation," I say, not wanting this concept to derail our progress so far.

"All of this will depend on your plant's heijunka concepts," says Josh. Heijunka is the Japanese concept of production levelling and schedule sequencing. This concept sets the pace for production smoothening, by redistributing the work in the assembly line cells. Then, each cell is work balanced, and can complete the assigned work within the specified cycle time.

"Sure," agrees Tom.

"Tom, these are big changes. When do you want to take it to the board for approval?" I ask.

"I want to do this right away. I will talk to marketing and send you my presentation so far. You can include the limit variation for the suppliers within the freeze period," he says.

"Let's present this at the annual board review on 1st October," I tell Tom. "We have two weeks in between, where I can get feedback from all stakeholders."

I ask Josh to join me at 3pm for my call with Neil as he heads out of my office.

I finish several calls after lunch, and I look at my watch. Time for my call with Neil. Josh joins me in my office.

Josh is excited to interact with Neil. I dial Neil's number. Neil is full of energy and hearing Neil is energizing Josh. After a few pleasantries, we get down to the job at home.

I explain the two issues that I have. The first issue is understanding aggregation and is there a benefit for using it in production.

"When we started the Apollo mission, we were told that our chances of coming back alive was 50-50. We knew from the previous track record it could be worse."

"I admire the risk that the team put up with," says Josh.

"Sure. But I say the Apollo mission as a contrast to the Space shuttle program. By that time, we had a highly sophisticated mathematical model to predict risk."

"Called the PRAN, the probability risk assessment number, the shuttle was estimated at 1/100, that is one launch failure out of every hundred," he says.

"Why I bring this up, is the PRAN number is more meaningful when there is a larger sample size." he adds.

Being a poker player during my college days, "That is the law of large numbers. The more bets you make, the more you have a chance of meeting the average," I add.

"Exactly. In your case, the more the number of dealer requests that you combine it will average out with the law of large numbers," he says.

"However, since you must deal with three systems – Dealer requests for specific models, plant build capacity for specific models and supplier capacity for switching models to meet dealer requests, you are in a bind. It is like the theory of constraints. Your output is constrained by the narrowest orifice for the flow," adds Neil.

"Interesting. I never thought of it that way," I say. "Since Suppliers are the constraint for me, we limit the changes at the supplier."

Neil agrees with an emphatic "Yes". "I would recommend that you smooth out 5% volume change up and down, which adds to the 10% that you were holding on the supplier before."

"I know that your plant has quick changeovers through the paint shop. Please ensure that the paint shop does not become the bottleneck," adds Neil.

Our conversation continues and I want Neil's take on the law of collective mutualism.

"It sounds like that there is a collective drive in the supplier ecosystem," he says.

"How do you propose to bring this into a collective learning out from the supply base?" he asks.

"Josh and I were discussing if we can introduce a separate learning channel, with some dedicated Toyonda resources, such as a budget and some manufacturing experts. They will help suppliers solve problems. The suppliers will have to present their findings at an internal supplier forum, so that all suppliers can learn," I say.

"Jishuken is a common style of self-learning in Japan today. You should call this channel as Jishuken, as well," he adds.

We wrap up the call, with the plan of meeting Neil during my visit to his glider club during one of these weekends.

After the call, Josh requests me to catch him up next time Neil is in town. I tell him that I will try.

When Josh leaves, I update the Supply Chain philosophy with three lines. These are additions to our philosophy.
- OEM and Suppliers as one Supply Chain
- Variety reduction
- Lean journey

I make a mental note that this updated Supply Chain philosophy should be presented to the supply base to create alignment.

Chapter 11: Steve deals with Supplier capacity
Global Motors HQ, Michigan
September 14, Monday

It is early Monday morning. I reached the office a few minutes ago and just sat down at my desk with my coffee, when the phone rings. It is Sammy Baker, the plant manager from the Ohio Plant. He is on a conference call with Sanjeev and he voices his frustration over how the new launch is not going well, because the supply base is not able to deliver at the pace that was promised.

"The supplier promised ramp up is not coming on time", chimes in Sanjeev.

"Why is there a gap?" I ask.

"That is the million dollar question," adds Sanjeev.

"I would like to find out more details," I concur with Sammy. "Who is your point person in central supply chain that is assisting you with your supply issues?"

"My team is working with Chuck Rainer," says Sammy with weariness in his voice.

"Let me review this and get back to you," I promise them.

I reach out to Chuck Rainer, to find out the details.

"Hello Chuck, I just had a call from Sammy Baker. He is concerned about the launch delays," I say. "Can you meet me in my office?"

"Sure Steve, I will be there in five" he says and joins me at my office in a few minutes.

"What is going on? Why are the suppliers not able to meet delivery volume rate during ramp up?" I ask the question that Sammy posed to me.

"The supplier demonstrated her ability to produce at the required rate during our pre-launch trials" says Chuck, explaining the background details.

"In this case, the *run-at-rate* demonstration was 50 jobs per hour. Our pre-production approval process, PPAP requires her to demonstrate meeting this target at this production rate during multiple days of pre-production trials," he continues. "so that she can show the run-at-rate confidence across multiple shifts day and night."

"So, what happened. Why this problem now?" I ask unknowingly.

"I have been in contact with the supplier throughout the weekend. In fact, one of my engineers is at the supplier site now," he says. "There are some issues at the supplier, when they are changing the line over from one product to another."

"How long is the change over time," I ask quizzically.

"About one to four hours," he says quickly.

"Chuck, Chuck, Chuck. That is not acceptable. First of all, that wide of variation is not good. Is this an estimate or do you have measured data on the changeover time?" I ask surprised.

"Secondly, why was the changeover time not documented during PPAP. And the third question is a major one, is that this amount of changeover time is still manageable and should not slow down the output rate. The plant is still at ramp-up mode, that means that we are far from full capacity. The supplier should not be struggling now," I say.

I am not sure that all the cards are on the table. So, we call the supplier CEO, Judy. Judy along with her production manager cannot pinpoint the source of the issue.

"We have recently started supplying additional components from the same line. We are looking into it," says Judy.

Chuck agrees to follow-up with the plant engineers and come back at the end of the day.

I can't imagine the issue to be a new one. "The last product launch was six months ago. Is there a lesson learned database from that one?" I ask Chuck.

He does not know that one exists. So, I make a mental note that we need one.

After Chuck leaves, I remember the weekend's conversation with Neil. Neil was able to put everything in context. I want to reach out to him later today. Knowing that Neil is teaching a class today, I decide to text him rather than call him.

> **Me:** Neil, Good meet up last weekend. Hope you are back in Ohio now.
>
> I hear a ping with Neil's reply.
>
> **Neil:** Sure. Was fun, like the old days.
>
> **Me:** Would like to setup a consultation phone call with you today. What time will work for you?
>
> **Neil:** I am in a class now, and the students are taking a test. I will be free at 5pm, if that works for you.
>
> **Me:** Sure. I will call you at 5pm. Thanks.
>
> **Neil:** Talk to you then. Bye.

I remember that the Ontario plant had a recent launch. I must reach out to the Plant manager to find out how his production ramp up is going on. He is launching a family of trucks, with the first vehicle six months ago and the next vehicle is getting ready for launch now.

-The tale of two supply chains: Toyota and GM-

I reach out to him by phone. "G'Afternoon Art," I start the conversation when he answers.

"G'Afternoon, how is the Ohio product launch going?" he says.

"Good overall. But we have some difficulties with the supplier's ramp up," I say.

"Did you have a similar situation during the MDY200 vehicle launch in March?" I ask enquiring about his situation.

"Somewhat," he says nonchalantly. "We had a good launch. But two suppliers were constantly behind, until we were able to bring additional capacity."

"Was this a real problem or were the supplier's holding your ramp-up captive for additional money" I ask bluntly.

"Suppliers are constantly delaying their required investment, while the expect to collect their tooling advance from us on time," he says openly.

"So, this is a commercialization problem?" I ask quizzically.

"No, these two suppliers had some genuine difficulty. It seems that their capacity planning had some flaws," he says.

"What do you mean?" I ask surprised. "They had a demonstrated capacity, before we were at job 1."

"True. Somehow the capacity planning before launch, is not the same as the actual capacity at job 1," he says with a sigh. I can feel that there is a personal pain point in his launch.

"Do you have a database of supplier ramp up issues," I ask trying to get a bigger picture learning from his work. "You are launching multiple products in the vehicle family. I expect that you will have one."

"We have a launch issues database, that includes supply issues as well," he says covering a wide range of supplier issues.

"Can you sort by launch issues or other criteria" I ask him to understand the usefulness of a large list.

"Sure. It is sortable multiple ways," he confirms.

"How can my team and I access that database," I wonder openly.

"No problem," he agrees to my surprise.

"May be one more favor. If the database is stable, can I roll it out a read-only version to a larger audience, so that the Ohio plant can learn from your experience?" I ask.

"I don't see a problem. But please talk to the plant IT manager. Meanwhile, I will send him a note asking him to setup an account for you," he says.

"Is the launch ramp up your biggest issue? Or is it something else?" I ask his opinion.

"Our biggest problem is not launch, but April being truck month," he says nonchalantly.

"How come?" I ask surprised.

"The volume of sales in April is about 150% that of March. In fact, our sales for April through June is about the same as the rest of the nine months combined," he says showing a wild change in production throughput.

"I thought that August through October sales are high as well," I say trying to understand the magnitude of the volume swings.

"No August is about 110% but the second quarter is 150% each month," he says. "how do you manage the production flow at that time?" I ask wondering if he can build ahead since I don't believe that the supply chain has the capacity to stretch 150% and still be efficient.

-The tale of two supply chains: Toyota and GM-

"No, we don't know the mix, so we have to cancel all employee vacations in the 2nd quarter. All hands on deck," he says to my complete surprise.

"We need to see how the supply chain flexibility can be planned. Let me know when you are in town next time, we should talk about this," I say finally.

"I will be in Michigan for Thanksgiving. Hope to catchup with you at that time," he says.

"Are you headed to the Michigan – Ohio State football game," I ask, knowing fully well that he is a die-hard Michigan fan.

"No, I have tickets to the Michigan-Michigan State game in the previous week. But the Ohio State game is all sold out," he says.

"Hey, I have two tickets to the game. I will be travelling that week, so I would not be able to use it. You are welcome to it," I say, knowing fully well that he is going to jump for it.

"I would love it. Let me know how much and I will Venmo you the money." he says.

"If your database helps, then this would be my treat," I say.

"No, no. Let me know how much?" he says.

We wrap up the call. I grab a water bottle from the fridge and get back to my desk. Ping. I see an email from the Plant IT with a new account setup. Wow, he is quick.

Chuck returns to my office at 4:30pm.

"How can the situation be so different between their run at rate demonstration a few months ago and why they are struggling now?" I ask Chuck again.

We review the supplier's production process. Their production cell cycle times are varying wildly. I email a copy of the production process diagram to Neil.

-The tale of two supply chains: Toyota and GM-

It is 5pm, and I dial Neil's number. I have asked Chuck to stay so that he can gain some perspective on the issue.

Neil joins the skype call. I am surprised at his energy level given his past retirement age.

After pleasantries, we get down to business.

I introduce Chuck to Neil. Neil is excited to have an engineer join the meeting.

"Do you know?" says Neil. "A pessimist sees a glass half empty...... An optimist sees the glass half full, while an engineer sees the glass twice as big as it needs to be," he adds.

Chuck is all smiles, that Neil likes Chuck's participation.

"Did you see the notes that I sent you?" I ask Neil. Neil just received them and is going through them as we speak. There is a short silence and he comes back on the skype.

The skype connection is very erratic today.

"What is the purpose of this plan," Neil questions me.

"We are expecting the supplier to demonstrate that the assembly cells that he has installed can deliver quality products, at the rate that we need for our vehicle assembly line," says Chuck.

"So, do you think that this plan delivers it?" he asks.

"We are finding some gaps. Supplier can show jobs per hour or JPH achieved at the rate, in preproduction trials. But he is behind now," I say stating the obvious.

"What do you think causes the difference?" Neil asks Chuck and I.

"The supplier's jobs per hour is varying widely," I say.

"because....," Neil prompts us.

-The tale of two supply chains: Toyota and GM-

"Some production cells are very stable in their cycle time, but some are changing substantially," I say after a thinking for a minute.

"Correct. What is the difference between the stable cells and the varying cells?" he asks us, as a follow up.

There is a silence and I can hear the distant chatter of the nighttime cleanup crew arriving.

"The stable cells are dedicated to Global Motors production. The varying cells are shared cells, which support other companies as well," says Chuck finally.

"Good. Now you have a clue," says Neil.

"Your overall equipment usage is high. In the 95%. That is good for keeping the production lean and the costs low. But is bad for managing throughput. Once you are behind, you don't have free machine time to catch up," says Neil.

"Secondly, your line is well balanced. But there are two bottlenecks cells. These are production cells that are running at full capacity, but need their full time capacity to process parts, since they are operating close to 100% of the time," he adds.

"You need a buffer of ready to go stock in front of the bottleneck stations, so that they never go idle," he continues.

"Wow, that is a lot to absorb" says Chuck.

"Should I repeat.... It is high equipment usage rate and bottleneck stations" says Neil.

"No. I got it," says Chuck.

"Thirdly, track record. This is just an observation. You have a track record for the supplier that covers only one week. You need multiple weeks of historical data to ensure a TRACK RECORD," says Neil.

We wrap up the call and Chuck brings a stack of reports to review which suppliers have capacity and which are struggling to meet demand. Looking at that pile, I call Debbie to let her know that I will be late for dinner.

Chuck and I review a sample of suppliers and find a few more suppliers with such history. By 8pm, we have reviewed about 30 suppliers and found a total of five supplier with such a history.

Chuck leaves my office, promising to review the rest. I open my outlook calendar to review the events for this week. I see George's staff meeting tomorrow, with "Tesla" as the agenda. *With a high flying stock, I wonder if there is a new electric vehicle product announcement in the horizon.*

Tesla has been a point of discussion in many Automotive company board room these days.

-The tale of two supply chains: Toyota and GM-

Supply Chain Management

Chapter 12: Tesla versus Everybody
September 15, Tuesday
Global Motors HQ, Michigan

It is 8:30am Tuesday morning and I am walking out of George's weekly staff meeting. Today we discussed the profitability of the Electric and Hybrid programs. Tesla is red hot in the marketplace and our electric vehicles are laggards. We need some quick answers.

JP Olenzek, the Marketing Director catches up with me as we walk out

"What do you think of the Electric program? How can Tesla make money on its small volume sales?" he asks me bluntly.

"Good question!" I say emphatically. "Not long ago, I had asked the same question to a Supply Chain expert. My question was how does a company like Tesla manage a small volume production?"

"His answer was three pillars. The first was hyper manufacturing," I explain. "Hyper manufacturing or giga factory is where the entire factory has to go digital. This adds flexibility to the product development and the build."

"What do you mean by flexibility?" ask JP puzzled. "So, Engineering can develop new processes and materials continuously. These materials are incorporated into the next build," I say capturing the essence of what Neil had told me earlier.

"Does that mean a continuously evolving bill of material?" he asks.

"No, the bill of material, or the BOM as they call it, is not different vehicle to vehicle. But the BOM drives the build from batch to batch. They can make part changes quickly and incorporate into the next batch of vehicle in a matter of weeks, as opposed to a matter of months in traditional manufacturing situations," I explain.

"That is an extremely agile supply chain. Is that feasible?" he asks.

"That's good. You identified the second pillar. It is a lean-agile supply chain. A quick change is a good and a bad thing. It is good when design evolves with manufacturing and testing. It is bad when the parts cannot be validated as quickly as the change," I say explaining further.

"So, there is a higher customer risk?" he asks enquiringly.

"There could be, if the systems are not in place to drive the right results. However, Tesla manages the risk well," I add.

"Does anyone else do such a rapid change to the BOM today?" he asks.

"Yes and no," I confirm. "Most vehicle manufacturers do not allow such changes. But small vehicle manufacturers, especially like the Great wall motors and other in China, have done similar BOM management. In the US, big truck manufacturers, such as Navistar and AutoCar make such a controlled change more often than the vehicle manufacturers."

"Interesting. So being a small manufacturer helps in this situation," he summarizes.

"Maybe. It is how you manage the product risk that is important," I say contrasting his summary.

"And the third leg to this low volume production run is additive manufacturing. Some parts will be made by melting powder together to create new parts," I explain further. "This lets them make their own parts for small components that they can't outsource competitively."

"So, the entire supply chain becomes local," says JP.

"Yes, for some key elements. However, these are the guiding principles for the Tesla program," I say finally summarizing Tesla's situation. "There are several low volume manufacturing strategies to build on these principles to reach breakeven."

"So, tell me JP. How is the market for electric cars?" I ask him.

"Electric vehicles are selling the world over. It is especially popular in China and many countries in Europe like Norway. Here in the US, it is popular in California and on the East Coast," he explains.

"A wide market. Impossible to ignore," I concur.

"These electric vehicles are selling at two distinct price points" he says putting this in context.

"One is the premium price point, where Tesla market is red hot. We have better technology and we should be driving that market," he continues.

"What does Tesla do that the others did not do?" I ask.

"At this premium price point, there is the Volt, a hybrid and Bolt, the electric. Volt was introduced at the Detroit auto show in January 2007, a few short months after Tesla announced the electric roadster priced over $100000. The Volt was discontinued in 2019. But the Bolt priced at around $37500 is still selling well," he explains.

"Selling well. But not a runaway seller?" I prompt him.

"Yes. In my opinion, a premium electric should be sold in a premium marque. So, I think that if the Volt or the Bolt was sold as a Cadillac or Lexus, it would have been very popular rather than as a Chevy brand," he agrees.

"Why is that?" I am surprised.

-The tale of two supply chains: Toyota and GM-

"It has to do with the customer profile. A premium customer is one that is open to new product technology and is willing to take on product risk as an early adopter," he continues.

"Here is a profile of a Tesla customer, taken from the book, The SMART Supply Chain" he says.   He then shows me his notes.

Segment Profile for Tesla Customers

General	Demographic
• **Region:** North America, Asia, Europe • **Location:** Urban & Semi urban (high) & Rural (moderate) • **Age:** 30+ • **Gender:** Male and Female	• **Occupation:** Working professionals Executives, Senior Managers • **Loyalty:** First time, Loyalists

Behavioral	General
• **Benefits sought:** Environmentally friendly, Perception of environmentally friendly, Status, Life time cost effectiveness • **Personality:** Determined & Ambitious • **User status:** Potential users, Nonusers and first time users	• **Social class:** Middle class, Upper class • **Lifestyle:** Early adopter, aspirational

"It looks like the electric and the hybrid car buyers prefer to think of themselves as unique," he says. "In focus groups, these customers called themselves as Volt or Bolt buyers, and not as Chevy buyers."

"In other words, they consider themselves a part of a luxury marquee, and there was no carryover benefit for the Chevy brand" I chime in.

He nods his head in agreement.

"But I see many Japanese brands selling electrics as base vehicle, such as under Toyota and Honda badge, rather than as Lexus or Acura," I ask a little bit confused.

"The Japanese car buyers prefer the mass market brands, like Nissan, Toyota and Honda. But the American car buyers prefer new technology to trickle down from the luxury brand to the mass market brand at that price point" he says. "We did not anticipate that shift," he adds.

"The real price point for the mass brand is what we are selling in China today. We have a joint venture in China that sells electric cars for around $8000. We will reintroduce that product back into the US as a mass market brand," he confirms the strategy.

"So are you saying that Tesla is starting from a luxury marque and then planning to move down market, the common American story of new technology starting out as a premium," I say finally starting to understand the market.

"Electric cars are here to stay the world over. The Paris climate accord envisions the first wave of electric cars at high volume will be around the year 2035," he summarizes.

"I read that Tesla recently merged its solar energy division with Tesla Automotive. How does this play?" I ask.

"This moves Tesla's mission from accelerating 'the advent of sustainable transport' to accelerating 'the world's transition to sustainable energy.' Something to watch," he says.

"You think that Tesla is angling for different synergy with this merger," I prod him.

"Yes. That is possible," he says.

"Let me call Sammy Baker. He is not a proponent of the Electric cars. I want to understand his perspective," I say.

I call Sammy and he comes on the line. Sammy is delighted that the Supplier issue tracker from the Ontario plant is helping his plant to proactively review supplier issues.

"I am glad that I was able to get that database rolled out to you," I say approvingly. "JP is here with me and I wanted to get your take on the future of electric vehicles."

-The tale of two supply chains: Toyota and GM-

"I really don't get this concept," says Sammy. "Several companies have launched electric vehicles in the past few years. Electric cars do not have the fuelling infrastructure to take them for long distance. I remember the first car that the company gave me for a test drive, I commuted during the week from home to work with no problems. I charged the car at home every day. However, that weekend, we went to Lansing for the State fair. The car ran out of juice on the way back and I had to get a tow to get back home."

"That is range anxiety," says JP.

"You have to constantly watch your battery gauge," I confirm.

"Yes Steve. Most electric car drivers watch their battery gauge. They don't travel far away from the charging stations. That is range anxiety," says JP with a smile.

"What about our strategy last year. We introduced hybrid cars, that had a gasoline engine add-on to extend the range until we get to a gas station," asks Sammy.

"We were just talking about the Volt hybrid," I add.

"The market is not going to hybrids," says JP. "It is going to electrics."

"Is it because of goddamn Tesla," ask Sammy sarcastically.

"Not particularly," he says. "Hybrids have an electric motor and a gasoline engine. That makes it expensive for the mass market," confirms JP. "However, the electric vehicle customer is more interested in being an early adopter, than wanting a hybrid."

"So, I suspect that the Cadillacs and Lincolns will be dedicated to electric drivelines to compete in the upmarket," I say understandingly.

"Yes. That is the idea," he concludes.

-The tale of two supply chains: Toyota and GM-

"Since the battery cost is high, our product strategy starts at high end. And moves downstream. However, we will start at the mass market end with our China like product and move upstream as well," he concludes.

"Also, I expect that a hybrid car, that has an electric motor and the add-on gasoline range extender will be discontinued in the future, since it does not fit the premium market," I say.

"I expect that all the automakers will make that choice sooner or later," he concludes.

I should discuss this at the next supply chain round table, I think to myself.

-The tale of two supply chains: Toyota and GM-

Supply Chain Management

Chapter 13: Supply Chain Round Table
September 18, Friday
University of Michigan, Ann Arbor, Michigan

Today I am at the University of Michigan Business School Auditorium. I arrive backstage, and the producer informs me that the round table show goes on air in 10 minutes.

"Hello Steve," I hear a voice and turn around to see Jeff Easley, the CEO of Magna Corporation. Jeff and I had been on-and-off golf buddies over the past 5 years.

"Hello Jeff, I see that they are letting SEC football fans into Big 10 territory," I say jokingly.

"Steve, I have not seen you in the golf course this season. What gives?" he asks.

"Travel schedule has been tight. I spent most of this summer travelling back and forth to Germany on business," I say brightly.

"I have some concerns about our supply structure. I would like to catchup with you after the roundtable," he says with a concern in his voice.

"Sure. Let's do it," I say, confirming his request.

Jeff and I walk on to the stage and are greeted by the moderator, Professor Joe Chen.

"Welcome to the round table. I would like to introduce the guests today," starts Joe.

"Our first guest is Steven Radue, the VP at Global Motors, who has a distinguished career in Supply Chain. Welcome to the show," he adds.

"Thank you, Joe. I am happy to be here," I say.

"And the second guest is Jeff Easley, the CEO of Magna Corporation. Magna is a top 10 supplier with expertise in components manufacture and in contract vehicle assembly in Europe and Asia. Welcome to the show," he says.

"Thank you," says Jeff.

"Our first question to Steve. The Auto industry has been a staple of the State of Michigan. But can you tell me the impact of the Auto Industry in the Supply Chain structure across the country and across the globe," says Joe.

"The top five automakers spend more than $300 Billion dollars in sourcing every year, just in the US. If you include the supply base, it is easily many times that," I start.

"We have made strategic investments in logistics and tracking of the goods move. Each of our factories typically has more than hundred trucks and rail cars in or out every day. So, our shipments are tracked by GPS and RFID tags on the trucks and in the warehouse. This helps the digital sequencing of parts when they arrive at the assembly line," I say explaining the Auto industry's contribution to logistics technology.

"Our factories have grown smarter and our new factories follow industry 4.0 standards, with smart automation," I add.

"Please explain, what is industry 4.0?" asks Joe.

"In the last two centuries, we have had three industrial revolutions. Each revolution had a key ingredient. A disruptive new technology, whether it is was the steam engine, the invention of the assembly line or the invention of the computer," I explain. "These technologies have revolutionized the way things were done, not just affect productivity and efficiency in a peripheral way. Now, we have digital technologies that are driving the fourth revolution, industry 4.0 with smart factories."

"Can you give us an example," asks Joe.

"In our new machine shops, all the new machining centers have a self-diagnosis protocol. If the machine vibration indicates an abnormality, the machine will run a self-test. If it is still a no go, the machine will send an alert to the maintenance department," I say. "So, the machines are not just smart enough to understand their contribution, but also interface with the system to call for help, when they are not."

"It is interesting that they are almost human like," says Joe.

"Exactly. Now coming back to the flow down benefits from our supply chain strategies. Supply Chain specialty companies have created new tracking utilities for moving goods for all industries using many of the elements that our Automotive Supply Chain professionals have created," I add.

"Yes, that has been a milestone in Supply Chain," confirms Joe.

Turning to Jeff, he asks, "Now Magna has been in a new space. You have expertise in component manufacture. But you have created a new business for assembling electric cars. How does this work?"

"The idea of contract assembly is the economies of scale. For small automakers the investment in manufacturing electric cars may not payoff since the volume for spreading the expenses is low," says Jeff.

"So, we have created two locations, one in Europe and one in China, where we can build electric cars based on the Automakers design," he adds.

"Does that business conflict with working with larger automakers on parts supply?" asks Joe enquiringly.

"No, we have not developed a consumer identifiable brand name. We do not intend to sell cars as Magna. So, we are just an enabler for kickstarting the electric car market," says Jeff breezily.

"We have built energy efficient factories that can produce up to 50000 cars for these small automakers," adds Jeff.

"Smaller companies such as Tesla?" I add.

"No, Tesla has a unique build strategy as you know with their own giga factories," says Jeff.

Then turning over to me, Joe asks, "That is a good seg way to our next topic. Talking about energy efficient factories. What steps have you done for reducing your carbon footprint in factories?"

"We are aiming to be carbon neutral in our Asian factories by the end of this year," I say.

"How about the US factories?" asks Joe.

"We want to complete the carbon planning for the newer Asian factories this year. In the US, we have created some unique concepts. One is the green roof initiative at one of the oldest factories in the Metro area. We have planted 400 thousand square feet of sedum and succulent plants on the roof, that has cut our heating expenses by half", I say.

"At the end of the year, we will have a major plan for the US factories carbon footprint," I say continuing our commitment to the environment.

We wrap up the round table. Joe comes up to Jeff and me, to thank us for the participation.

"I wish we can have more industry folks that can shed some inside light," says Joe looking at me. "Sure Joe, I can recommend some of my colleagues to participate" I say knowing Joe. Joe was my business professor several years ago, when I came into Michigan for my management degree.

On the way out, Jeff and I grab some coffee at the Starbucks counter and sit down.

"Steve, you guys are killing us with the late engineering changes," says Jeff, starting up the conversation of what has been bothering him in his business.

"What do you mean. I thought the suppliers make a killing in overcharging for late changes," I say jokingly.

"No, no. We don't make a penny on those changes," he says adamantly.

"We try to estimate the cost of the change so that we can close the cost gap. But many times, we are caught in the mandatory limits and wind up eating way too much costs," he says summarizing his pain points.

"Interesting. We were talking about this last week at the office. Our projects are in trouble over these costs," I say trying to see the other side of the picture.

Finishing up the coffee and needing to hurry back to the office I say, "Send me some details so that I can get to the bottom of this issue."

On the way back to the office, I call Jennifer Ming, the Program Director.

"Hello Jennifer, how are you doing?" I start.

"Hello Steve, I am doing good. I heard that you were headed to the Supply Chain Round table at the University of Michigan. How did that go?" she asks.

"Went well. In fact, I am on the way back from there. I was talking to one of the producers earlier, and he wanted to have more program folks come and join them some time. Are you open to addressing the students at the Business School?" I ask her, knowing that she would be an ideal candidate.

"Sure. That sounds like a good idea," she says.

"That's good. Anyway, I had an interesting conversation with Jeff from Magna about late engineering changes. It was a surprise for me that he was complaining that he is losing money. Can you catch me up on what's going on?" I ask.

"I will meet you at your office in another half hour. Will that work for you?" she asks.

"Sure, I should be there by then. Thanks," I say.

-The tale of two supply chains: Toyota and GM-

I park my car and make it back to my office and find Jennifer waiting for me there. We sit at the side table near the end of the office. She opens her computer and projects onto the TV screen to explain the details.

"You see that our vehicle projects are 48-month projects from concept approval to job 1 production," she says setting up the background.

"36 months before production is program approval gate, where the suppliers have submitted quotes for the new designs that we need. At that gate, the supplier has firm pricing and we have a program budget to execute a new product," she continues.

"But during the testing phase leading up to midway of the project, we may discover new issues," she adds briskly.

"Such as...", I prod.

"In the midsize vehicle project, we did a crash test in 24 months, and discovered that the engine components poke into the passenger compartment during the crash," she says.

"That is a safety concern. So that will trigger a design change," I add understandingly.

"Yes, so that change to the engine in that case cost us a 27% increase in our tooling cost" she says gently.

"Whew. That is substantial for a single change. But why is supplier not happy with the change?" I ask being surprised.

"I can't see why the supplier is not happy," she says also being surprised.

We walk through about 20 such examples of cost changes. In fact, eighteen of these cost changes are tied to late engineering changes. Jenny, my secretary, pokes her head in the office to remind me that our scheduled call with Neil is in a few minutes.

"Jennifer, this would be a perfect opportunity to discuss this cost changes with Neil," I say.

Jennifer stays on while I dial Neil's phone number.

"Good afternoon Neil," I say.

"Good afternoon Steve" says Neil.

After pleasantries, we get started. "Neil, I have Jennifer here who heads the program and new product launch departments. We have some questions on the effect of late engineering changes," I say moving over to the purpose of today's call.

Jennifer explains the list of changes and the cost impact on the project. Neil listens intently and then explains.

"You know the cost impact of the late changes is easy to extract by the rule of thumb," he says.

"When I was advising NASA on the space shuttle, the original cost of the space shuttle was $8000 per pound of payload. Now space shuttle is a reusable launch vehicle, so the cost was supposed to be cheaper than the Proton rockets from before," he says.

"Unfortunately, due to Challenger's delay and the increased safety rules later on, the cost of the shuttle skyrocketed to $27000 per pound of payload," he says continuing the explanation.

"The post project review estimates that the cost of the project would have been less than $20000 if these rules were in place before the start of the project," he adds.

"How is it possible to have the ongoing expense be over 130% of the cost?" asks Jennifer.

"Let me explain with a more common example. If you were building a starter house, let's say that the cost of the house could be one hundred thousand dollars," he explains his example.

"If you decide to add a sun-room or extend your dining room after the house is planned or more commonly after it is built, the house will cost more than 130% of the original cost," he continues.

"Oh. I can see that," I say and Jennifer agrees.

"So even though, I as a homeowner am spending 130%, the contractor is not making any more money per hour, that he or she is spending on the project," confirms Jennifer.

"Yes. So, my rule of thumb is that if your design changes are done before print release, then the cost is within base cost. Design errors could cost five times for the change, if done during industrialization, ten times if done at supplier equipment run-off, 20 times if during ramp up, and 50 times if there is a field return," he says explaining his rule of thumb.

"So, your point is to do a full freeze on the design, before supplier tool up," I say trying to draw a conclusion.

"Exactly," he agrees.

"I call this cost escalation as a shadow chart, that the length of the cost impact is longer, the later the change happens. Much like the length of an evening shadow, the later it is," he says.

"These changes are difficult to manage," I say thinking the complexity of the Engineering task. "However, the more you freeze, the better the cost," concludes Neil.

-The tale of two supply chains: Toyota and GM-

Chapter 14: Kevin and Steve go to glider training
September 19, Saturday
Drive to Columbus, Ohio

Finally, the weekend is here. Steve and Debbie will join Donna and I for a trip to Columbus, Ohio this weekend. Debbie hired a babysitter for the weekend, and we meet at Steve's house on Friday night to pack the car for the trip.

Donna and Debbie are very excited to attend the Lithopolis Honey Festival near Columbus. Besides the honey festival, Steve and I would also have a half a day to catch up with Neil at his glider club near Columbus.

Saturday starts up early. Debbie and Donna are up at 4 am and are baking up a storm. I can smell the aroma of fresh baked honey cookies and honey cakes when I get up at 5am. The gals want to head out to the National honey bakeoff competition at Lithopolis. Debbie gave us some samples that she had baked earlier after dinner last night. The golden crust and the moist flavor were an instant hit with the family. Debbie used natural honey for the pies that will be ready in the morning for our trip.

We leave early in the morning for our drive to Columbus. The road trip is fun, and we reach the festival in time for the early registration. I help the gals setup a sampling booth for the judges, while Steve is busy with the camera. He is a whiz when it comes to showing the texture of the food in the pictures. I can see the shades of golden brown crust of the pies, that were baked to perfection. By 10:30am the festival grounds are busy with hundreds of visitors clamoring at the stalls and the start of the honey cookoff demonstrations.

At about 11am, after the gals are setup, Steve and I take off to the glider club to visit Neil. The club is a short drive away. Arriving at the club hanger, Steve is enamored with the several small engine aircraft on display. Steve and I are looking at the newer planes, when Neil catches up with us.

"Glad that you could make it," says Neil.

"This was the perfect weekend," says Steve. "Debbie and Donna have always wanted to come to the honey festival. And we have an opportunity to make it to the club."

"How about you Neil?" I ask. "I heard that you had some medical procedure last week? Is everything OK?"

"I had a minor work done last week. I am feeling fine now," he says cheerfully.

"Looks like a wide array of planes here. I was expecting just gliders," I say looking around.

"We have a full flying club here besides our glider club," says Neil pointing to the training aircraft parked next to the gliders.

"Ah… Let me show you what we have done with the engine that Steve, you sent me," he continues.

Neil directs us to a nearby hanger with a new plane assembly. He gets into the cockpit and starts the engine. The engine is quiet, but we can see the power in the display gauge.

"Lots of power, for a small aircraft," says Steve.

"We can reduce the maximum power by throttling it. But can you imagine, this engine puts out twice the power of the old engine. But weighs less and fits into the same space," says Neil.

Sarah, our flight instructor joins us, as we get ready for the lessons.

"Sarah, you sound very familiar. Where have I seen you before?" I ask quizzically.

"Steve and Kevin. I know you both. I am the coordinator for the IHS Markit, the Purchasing Manager's index," she says.

"Yes. I send out my economic outlook forecast every month to you," says Steve.

"Correct. Between Kevin and you, both of you represent 50% of my automotive outlook for the Purchasing Managers Index," she says confirming her role.

"That's an impressive volume," says Neil with a knowing smile.

"How does the outlook look like for next month?" I ask wondering how a glimpse into the future will look like.

"We are compiling the numbers. You will have to wait and see," she says with a smile. The index details are always kept secret till the publication.

With that she takes us to the two Blanik L-23 aircrafts ready for our glider lessons. The two gliders have dual controls for the instructor and the student. The dash has all the instruments of a real aircraft, even without the engine.

With a tow start, we are in the air. We are airborne for about half an hour. And what an exhilarating time it is. By the time we are back at the hanger, it is around 3pm. Neil walks back to join us as Steve shares some of Debbie's honey baked cookies with him.

Our conversation turns to National honey month.

"Did you know that bees have one of the best circadian rhythms?" says Neil.

"Circadian rhythm...... the daily body clock?" I ask.

"Yes. The bees have a well-tuned rhythm. They start the day at the same time, and if they have discovered a honey field, they trace back their path at the same time every day," he says explaining the bees' daily cycle. "Their internal body clocks are so tied to the 24 hour circadian pattern, that NASA did several experiments on bees to test their body clock" he continues.

"Didn't NASA send some bees into space?" interrupts Steve.

"NASA sent 3400 bees on the space shuttle challenger as a part of student experiments. The weightlessness didn't bother the worker bees. They produced a perfect honeycomb and the

-The tale of two supply chains: Toyota and GM-

queen laid 35 eggs. The honeycomb was 30 square inches, just about the same size as they would have been on earth," says Neil.

"The point is that Supply Chain is like a circadian clock. Incoming material and outgoing material would have to work like clockwork for an effective Supply Chain to perform," he continues.

"Your incoming material, plant operation and outgoing vehicles are a part of the circadian rhythm. Every day you have a few hundred rail cars and trucks come in and leave the facility. Your scheduler stays on the top of it. If the schedule is disrupted, there is twice the work, just keeping up with the change," adds Neil.

"Neil, is it better to have a standalone purchasing function or combine it with material planning and logistics group?" asks Sarah.

"Some companies have found synergy between Purchasing and MP&L. Others have found synergy with Purchasing and Supplier Development Engineering. It is really based on the corporate culture where they fit in," says Neil explaining the supply chain structure.

"How is your supply chain journey going overall?" he asks us.

Steve and I nod our heads.

"Progress is good, I take it. But remember that your measurables is what makes the progress stick. What gets measured gets done," he concludes.

We wrap up our trip to the glider school.

As we walk back to the car, I notice Steve walking with a slight limp. "Are you Ok?" I ask him. "Just made a hard landing. No worries," he says.

"Hope to catch up in Michigan next time," says Neil as he waves to us on the way out.

As we head out, Neil reminds us that we will meet at Tuscan Grill, in the Columbus Easton Mall for dinner. We, then head over to the Lithopolis festival to spend some time with our spouses.

-The tale of two supply chains: Toyota and GM-

Supply Chain Management

Chapter 15: Death of a legend
September 22, Tuesday
Beaumont Hospital, Michigan

It is 8am on this cold Tuesday morning. Debbie had woken me up last night, with a phone call. I can still hear the urgency in her voice when she had called me. Steve had passed out on the top of the stairs and had tumbled down as they were headed to the bedroom last night.

Now we were waiting in the hospital for the diagnosis. *Why did Steve blank out? Was he OK, when he was limping home after the glider flight?*

While we are at the waiting room, Debbie brings me Steve's phone. "I think you should take this call," she says. I look up the phone and recognize Neil's number.

"Hello Neil," I start up.

"Hello Steve," says a female voice on the phone.

"This is Carol, Neil's wife".

"Hello Carol, I don't think that we have met. But good to talk to you," I say. "This is Kevin," I continue.

"Hello Kevin. I am sorry to let you know that Neil passed away in his sleep yesterday. I know that you all were planning to meet up soon," she says. "Neil used to talk about Steve and you all the time," she adds.

"Oh, gosh. I did not know. We just met him and he was his jovial self," I gasp for words.

"He was not keeping good health after the minor heart surgery a few weeks ago," she continues.

"Is there anything that I can do to help?" I volunteer.

"We are in a state of shock, but Neil wanted to have his funeral private," she says.

"Sorry for your loss," I say. "He is a loss for us too," I add. After a few more brief words, she hangs up.

It is 10am, we are still waiting the results from Steve's visit from the MRI and X-rays. The doctor finally walks up and is looking to talk to Debbie. I join Debbie as the doctor starts up.

"You know that Steve had a serious incident with the fall. However, the good news is that he did not break any bones," says the doctor.

It sounds like a long silence as we wait for the doctor to continue.

"The bad news is that the concussion that he had suffered long ago, has affected his spinal chord," he says.

"What does that mean, doctor?", asks Debbie anxiously.

"He will be in a wheelchair," responds the doctor with a slight sigh. "He will need physical therapy. Over time, he may get better," he adds.

"Are you saying that there may be a possibility that he will not walk again?" I ask.

"That is a possibility as well," he adds somberly, shaking his head slightly.

"How is it possible for a concussion suffered in college to have an effect after these many years?" I ask with a heavy heart.

"Concussions are cumulative damage to the head. The long term implications are often times complications because the brain does not have a chance to fully recover before the next damage," he says. "Unfortunately, concussion was not taken seriously until about ten years ago," he adds.

The doctor then leaves us to continue his hospital rounds as we hurry to see Steve at his hospital bed.

It is now 8pm, I head over to the cafeteria to grab some dinner. The cafeteria is closed, and I pickup some eats from the vending machine and sit down. Donna joins me there.

"It has been a traumatic day," I tell her. "First Steve is diagnosed as a paraplegic and then Neil passed away," I say tearing up a bit.

Donna gives me a hug. "I know, you lost two of your mentors today. How are you handling it?," she asks.

"That is true. I have always been able to count on Steve, since highschool. Now I have to practice what I know," I say half cheerfully.

"Übung macht den meister, Practice makes the Master, isn't it what I heard Steve, Neil and you talk this past month?," she says.

She has a point.

-The tale of two supply chains: Toyota and GM-

Supply Chain Management

Chapter 16: Introducing Jishuken problem solving
September 24, Thursday
Toyonda HQ, Michigan

It has been several days since our return from Ohio. The idea of Jishuken learning network is now a major initiative.

Bill has been very supportive with the idea and has assigned six technical experts for the pilot activity. Our task is to demonstrate the value addition with this learning network process, so that we can reach full strength and spread the learning concept across the entire Supply Chain. Today is the first meeting from the Jishuken network.

As I walk out to the auditorium for the Jishuken network meeting, I see Tom's email.

From: Nakamura, Tom
Sent: September 24, 9:45 AM
To: Radue, Kevin
Cc: Plant Management Team
Subject: Annual Review preparation for the board

Hello Kevin:

Enclosed is the presentation for the annual review with the board. The following new proposals are included in this package.

1. Changes to Freeze-Thaw-Slush zones
2. Changes to the Standard vehicle spec packages – Economy, Deluxe and Luxury options
3. Deletion of low selling options
4. Incorporation of two cross docking facilities

I have reviewed the details with the plant and marketing stakeholders. If I have the supply chain support, I will submit this package for our annual board meeting. Please give me your feedback by COB on Friday, September 25.

-Tom Nakamura
Plant Manager
Mississippi Plant #1 & #2

I like Tom's detailed analysis and business case scenarios of why the change will be beneficial to the company. He monetizes the benefits of this change, with cost reductions in simplified procedures, quality improvement in changes. These benefits are weighed against the higher stress on dealers, that now must decide on a build specification freeze two weeks ahead of the prior plan. The dealer council has signed off on the cost benefit tradeoff.

This will make my supply chain job easier, I think to myself. I will send him a confirmation after I review the details with my team at my Friday staff meeting.

The auditorium is filled with supplier personnel. We have about 100 supplier personnel on site and about an equal number of others online today for the kickoff of the Jishuken network.

David Joseph leads the team of Supply Chain technical experts to review the status of the lean implementation in small suppliers that have low production requirements. David Joseph takes the mic to start the conversation.

"Welcome the first meeting of the Jishuken network. The company has committed some resources which are free to the suppliers for problem solving. The only commitment from the suppliers is that they in-turn make a presentation of their learnings in this forum."

The tale of two supply chains: Toyota and GM

"Today we have three speakers. The first one is Dominique Stevens, the Production Manager from HVAC Technologies. Please welcome Dominque."

With an applause, Dominque joins David on the stage.

"Thanks for this opportunity to join in this unique network. As you may know, we are a small supplier and we had a working plan to get to our target productivity," says Dominique.

"This means that if they setup a dedicated assembly line for our volume requirement, the manpower will remain idle for part of the week," says Dominique. "Since we are a family owned business with a loyal workforce, we cannot hire and layoff our workforce continuously. This is not acceptable for our business plan."

"So what is your solution?" asks David, curious about the path they have taken.

"We have worked with Toyonda's experts and benchmarked two other small firms and two larger firms to see their details," says Dominique, opening a new avenue for learning for this network, one of open data sharing for solving problems.

"These companies have or have had a similar problem due to volume and manpower constraints. They are currently doing batch production, their cycle times show that they will complete their weekly production requirements in three to four days a week," he says.

"So, what do you recommend?" asks David.

"We recommend that they continue on the lean journey, specifically reduce the work in process inventory, but not switch to an assembly line right away," says Dominique.

"That is a radical change. How will they reach lean, if they delay this process now?" asks David.

"Lean is a journey. In the meantime, we recommend that they introduce in-process checks so that the parts leaving one station are quality ready for next station," says Dominique. "In our assembly layout, we expect that if we continue on the heijunka, we will reach a cycle time necessary for continuous production like an assembly line over a period of six months."

I smile to myself as I listen to the team presentation.

"How will you make the process checks more meaningful?" asks David.

"Product engineering has agreed to give us a nominal part, an actual cutout of production vehicles that we can fit our components, as we work on the in-process" says Dominique.

"Can you give us an example?" asks David.

"We supply air conditioning HVAC systems and we will fit the HVAC hose on the roof of an actual car to ensure the fit, before the part is approved for shipment," says Dominque.

"This kind of realistic gauging does two things. First it ensures the supplier manages the process and its quality at each station. Secondly the supplier becomes very familiar with the usage of the parts in a vehicle. A win..win" says David.

"And we will present our progress again in the next quarter," says Dominique.

"Their presentation, charts and figures are available for download from the SharePoint site. Thank you, Dominique," says David.

The second presentation is from Malachi Weissman on how to handle bottlenecks in the assembly line.

"Good morning everyone. Thanks for giving me this opportunity to present our learnings on bottlenecks from our Mexico plant."

"Earlier this month, we had a slow build due to a quality issue. We had difficulty to reach our production rate due to a bottleneck operation" says Malachi.

"Our brazing furnace cycle time was 55 seconds, while the remaining processes were operating at 40 seconds," he continues.

"That was your bottleneck process, so all the other processes were waiting for parts from brazing" says David summarizing the activity.

"Yes. So, we instituted the drum-buffer-rope scheme," says Malachi.

"What is that?" asks David.

"A drumbeat is the speed at which the process can deliver parts smoothly. Our drumbeat is one part every 55 seconds, since brazing was the slowest process in the line. Since the brazing furnace is midway in the sequence, every operator after the furnace is waiting for brazed parts for her operation" says Malachi.

"So, I understand the drumbeat, but what is the ROPE and BUFFER," asks David.

"Rope is the lead time, at which we have to trigger the previous parts, so that we have enough parts for the furnace. We start the operator after the furnace a little later, so that she can catch up with her speed at 40 seconds and her incoming parts at a slower speed due to the bottleneck," he says.

"What is the buffer?" asks David.

"Since the brazing furnace is the most expensive and longest operation in the plant, we don't want the operation to ever go idle," he says. "So, we have a buffer of parts, ready to go for the brazing furnace at all times, so that it is never starved for parts," he explains.

"So, using the logic of the drum-rope-buffer, you are able to plan the throughput of the line, so that you have no time wastage," says David, summarizing the presentation.

"Any other improvements that you were able to do to your line?" asks David.

-The tale of two supply chains: Toyota and GM-

"We had micro-stoppages before, where the line moves and stops. Now we have eliminated those" says Malachi.

"What are MICRO stoppages?" asks David quizzically. "Every time the line stops, we document why it stopped and what we had to do to get the line restarted. However, it the line stops for less than 55 secs, that is less than one drum beat we don't document such small stops that are productivity killers. These are micro stoppages," he summarizes.

So, what is your overall improvement?" asks David.

"We have a total of 15% improvement of throughput from drum-buffer-rope strategy and another few percentage points from micro-stoppage and other fine tuning. In total, we have 23% improvement," says Malachi.

"That is astounding. Give it up for Malachi and his team," says David. The team receives an ovation, as he steps down from the stage.

The third report out was from David himself. "We have made some changes to the Supply Chain framework triangles, based on our Jishuken learnings," says David. "As a constantly learning peer to peer network, we want to set up some guidelines and overall suggestions."

"So, Kevin has asked me to present the new guiding philosophy additions to our supply chain," he continues. "As you all know, our guiding philosophy is a part of the 4P pyramid. I have expanded on the philosophy to include the Automaker as a partner in supply chain, along with the process, people and problem solving," expanding on the guiding philosophy so that we can enable quick learning.

-The tale of two supply chains: Toyota and GM-

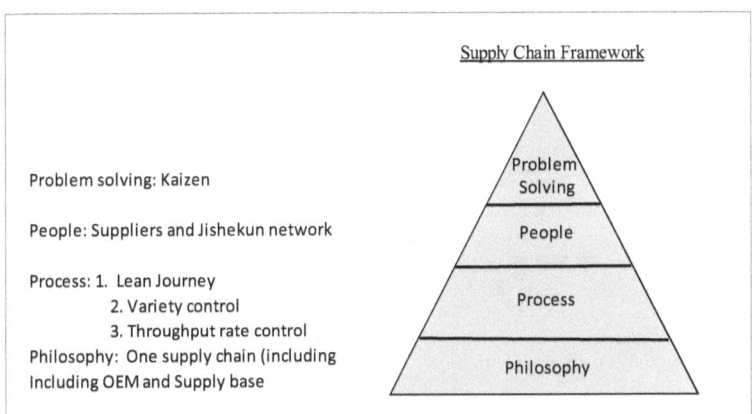

Final 4P pyramid

"This is the new Supply Chain framework," says David. "As we evolve as a supply chain, we will post new updates to this framework. Any questions?"

After a brief pause, "Thanks for your participation in the network."

-The tale of two supply chains: Toyota and GM-

Supply Chain Management

-The tale of two supply chains: Toyota and GM-

Chapter 17: Creating Performance Metrics

September 25, Friday
Toyonda HQ, Michigan

Today is my first staff meeting in my leadership role. I have invited the Shukkos and the buyers to my staff meeting.

"Good to have everyone here. Let's get started. In the past month, we have done some major changes. We have made some new processes and procedures," I start the meeting.

"I want to recognize the efforts of a few individuals. David Joseph has worked closely with Jonathan, Josh, and the Supply Chain community to present the first Jishuken learning results. Congrats to all three of you," I add.

After a brief applause, I continue. "David, do you want to say a few words?"

"It is a team effort, and each one of us had a crucial part to play. We have a few more people joining the team shortly as well" he says. "Thanks for all your support."

Josh and Jonathan echo in agreement.

"In the past month, we have solved two critical issues. One is that we have incorporated Theory of constraints to ensure that production line bottlenecks are handled. Lean process is driven by the lean journey and our Supply Chain framework has been updated. This will drive the future training plans with our teams and with our suppliers. We have made supplier work in process inventory reduction a priority," says David summarizing the lessons learnt through the Jishuken network.

"Good progress," I concur.

"Secondly, we have included a requirement for just-in-time pickup to be completed before the program approves the new supplier. A delay could signal some confusion and changes at job 1 date. This is also a process update," says Josh.

-The tale of two supply chains: Toyota and GM-

"We have quality improvements as well. We have approved line checks by location, new types of gauges and where to use light screens," says Jonathan.

"Great work all three," I say. "I believe that this new step is an opportunity for growth within the company. I firmly believe that growth does not happen without being grounded in the right metrics," I continue.

"Is there a metric that we need for the current actions," asks Josh.

"Yes," I say continuing the conversation. "Our normal metrics are based on being Forward SMART. You all know that SMART stands for metrics that are Specific, Measure-able, Attainable, Realistic and Timebound. The Forward element of our metric enables us to capture our lessons learnt into the process, so that the process does not stall at the same fault," I explain.

"So how do you measure being Forward," asks David.

"In this case, we need to put in place, changes for the process so that we don't reach the same stall point next time when we have a similar situation," I say explaining the need further.

"So, in the case of the Supply Chain framework, adding the changes to our philosophy at the bottom of the triangle is the lessons learnt and Forward SMART", says Jonathan.

"Not quite. If that Supply Chain framework, will ensure that the next person, next time will be able to solve that issue, before it is a problem, then you are right," I say about the strategic location for lessons learnt data.

"So, we may have to do some brainstorming to see if that is the right level of lesson for the next person," says Josh.

"Where will the lessons learnt capture make sense?" asks Jonathan.

"You may have to make some changes to the processes and procedures in addition to the framework," I say. "I will leave this as a follow-up subject for our next meeting. Please think about it and comeback with a plan."

"The second agenda item that I want to discuss today, is the change proposal for the supply chain. I have worked closely with Tom Nakamura on the supply and build strategy changes, that he plans to present to the strategy board," I explain the background. "There are four changes to the supply side for us. First is the change to the freeze timing to the build schedule"

"Oh, that is a welcome change" says Josh. "We can manage the incoming material better with an earlier freeze."

"What about the dealers wanting to make changes to their vehicles later in the production schedule?" asks Jonathan.

"Tom has their buyoff. If the quality improves by a couple of points, that is a welcome change for them" I say explaining Tom's email from yesterday.

"How does this affect quality?" asks Josh. "If the build is frozen earlier, then the incoming parts are delivered per schedule. This would create a more stable build plan and a better quality output," I summarize.

I see that the team agrees. So, we move to the next item from Tom's email. "Tom is eliminating some low selling options from the build mix," I explain. "He has created three standard packages, economy, deluxe and luxury for his builds. By this choice, some equipment, such as leather seats will be available only in luxury options."

"What if a customer wants to purchase an economy package with leather seats?" asks Becky. "If you are a unique customer then the dealer will install leather seats as an add-on," I say to capture Tom's logic.

"Is it not a loss for the company to redo seats?" asks Josh. "No, if it is less than 5% of the sales volume, then the company would charge the customer for the additional seat and would break even on the upgrade cost. Most economy customers do not take that option. Only about 5% or less are asking for it," I conclude.

"So, all low selling options are being eliminated?" asks Jonathan. "Yes, if it is less than 10 days-worth of sales a year," I conclude.

"How is the plant handling the new supplier pickups?" asks Josh.

"I am glad that you brought that up. Tom is requesting two cross docking stations for collecting incoming materials from the furthest suppliers," I explain the new initiative.

"That is a welcome change," says David.

"Yes, now our next batch of new suppliers can be covered with the existing truck fleet. We will be still at 85% utilization for the JIT pickup" I explain.

The team agrees that the Annual review has the full support of the Supply Chain. I will write to Tom to confirm that he has a good package and I support it fully.

We wrap up the staff meeting, with the plan to meet next week with more substantive plan for implementing new key metrics.

As I walk back to my office, I know that many managers will disagree with me, in developing the metrics along with the team. However, as Neil and I had a conversation last weekend, a radical forward measurement plan is one thing, but the engagement and the commitment to the measurement is key for success. So, I believe that the team should be involved in developing the metric to be committed to its execution.

I have a quick lunch at my desk, and then I head over to Bill's office. I have not met with Bill since the visit to the plant several weeks ago.

I find Bill at one of the temporary offices for visiting executives. He has a permanent office at each plant and spends his time at the temporary office when he is at the headquarters.

With a gentle knock, I enter his office. "Good Afternoon Bill. Are you ready for me?", I say.

"Yes, Kevin. Come on in. Is it 1pm already? Yes, let's get started. Take a seat," he says.

"How has your new role startup been going?" he asks.

"Very well, I think," I say. "We have just launched the Jishuken learning process and made some changes to the sourcing activities in the last two weeks."

"Sure. How has David, Josh and Jonathan been able to perform in their new assignments?" he asks about my broader support.

"I think that they have made good progress'" I say. "We had three presentations yesterday. Did you see it on the livestream on the corporate TV?"

"Sure, I was able to see it. Good work," he says. "Have you worked out the changes to the KPIs that you will track in your new role," he asks.

"I believe the Jishuken network should have a metric of never having to repeat the same fault within the supply base twice," I say.

"That is good. How will you ensure that the learnings are shared across the entire Supply Chain and followed through during problem solving?" he asks.

"I have added a contract page to the supplier agreement that if they participate in Jishuken, one representative will attend the presentation either on site or through live feed. Further they will roll out that lessons learnt into their organization," I say.

"OK. That is good," he says. "How about your other metrics?"

"As per the rolldown of your metrics, my team and I will have quality, cost or profit margin, development speed, lean productivity and manufacturing flexibility as metrics," I say.

"And any additions to the Supply Chain philosophy?" he asks.

I show him the Supply Chain framework that David and I have rolled out at the Jishuken network.

"One major addition is that we will allow the lean journey to be the driver instead on insisting on the first time leanness. This will allow our local supply base to gradually transition from batch production to one-piece flow over time," I say explaining our logic behind it.

"I expect that the transition plan is through the gradual reduction on work in process inventory," he says focusing on how our lean journey will happen.

"Yes. The forward metric will have equal weightage as the problem solution," I say, explaining the reward mechanism for people to attain their goals.

"That 50-50 split is going to be the toughest issue. You are going to credit someone only 50% of the reward for solving the problem now and tell them that if the problem does not repeat the next year that will get the next 50%?" he asks rather surprised.

"Yes. I see no other way to implement a robust lessons learnt plan. In fact, I got the team developing the metrics themselves. I will keep you posted on how we progress to a goal agreement" I say.

"The key expectation is that we will not manage the metrics, but the system that leads to results. So, this will lead people to solve the problem and improve the system. There will not be a rollercoaster ride of good years and bad years in problem solving," I say summarizing the plan.

"I like that. A good start to your work. Hope you can build on that," he says with a smile.

Heading back to my desk, I reflect on the continuous stream of issues that we have had to deal with in the past month. We have come a long way.

I pick up the phone to call Donna and remind her about the gala dinner this weekend.

-The tale of two supply chains: Toyota and GM-

Supply Chain Management

Chapter 18: Kevin & Steve at the Phi Delt dinner
5th Tavern, Bloomfield, Michigan
October 3, Saturday

Donna and I arrive with Steve and Debbie, by limousine for the Phi Delt fraternity dinner at the 5th Tavern at 5pm.

Steve and I had joined the Phi Delta fraternity when we were at college. Today, the Michigan Chapter is throwing a gala dinner in Bloomfield Hills, a suburban neighbourhood in Southeast Michigan. Neil was being honoured posthumously at this dinner.

Donna and I had gotten ready at around 4pm and drove over to Steve's house. Donna wore an elegant black dress, while I felt out of place in the tuxedo suit that I was wearing. Debbie and Steve were ready at the door. Debbie had arranged her mother to babysit all our kids at their place. Steve wore a hand tailored Laniori Italia suit, with a purple tie, while Debbie wore a purple dress. Steve looked comfortable in the wheelchair.

The fifth tavern dinner hall is packed with dignitaries. The Mayor, the Governor and several news anchors are at the social hour before dinner. At 6pm, the dinner is served, and the dinner speeches have just started. First up, it is the Governor. Later it is time for Steve's speech. Steve talks about the race in space during cold war and how it shaped America. He ends the speech and then assists the Governor in giving the Phi Delt lifetime award to Carol, Neil's widow.

After dinner drinks, I meet with Steve at the bar. "Congrats on the award", I say.

"Thank you. It is a longgg winded speech day today. Glad you survived it," he says jovially.

"So, you think that space is another frontier for competition," I say referring to his comments at the speech.

"Yes. In the 60s, space competition between US and Russia changed the cold war dynamics into a friendly competition," he says elaborating his thoughts.

"And you think that the corporations are the new face of international competition today," I say, acknowledging the current state of international diplomacy.

"Look at Russia and US, now our space competition has evolved into a coopetition, a cooperative competition. We are cooperating in the international space station and the future mars launch, while each country is developing its own private space travel companies," he says trying to expand the picture.

"Do you see the ability of coopetition in the auto industry?" I ask inquiringly.

"I see that new technology growth, such as in electric vehicle platforms, electric charging infrastructure and the fuel cell development would require pooling of resources and some joint ventures," he says nodding his head to emphasize his point.

"What do you think of supplier value?" I ask, trying to grasp the full impact.

"Suppliers can add immense value. It is up to you as an automaker to take advantage and unlock the value," he continues.

"Automakers are investing heavily in growth. How can the suppliers contribute to that growth?" I ask trying to comprehend the scope.

"Think about this. Let's take one area. New technology development, such as hydrogen fuelled vehicles. Automakers invest about $500 Billion in such new technology. The suppliers can magnify that resource by a factor of ten. So, I would ask, how can you not take advantage of this benefit" he concludes with a smile.

Helping his wheelchair cross the door threshold, I ask "What are you work plans going forward?".

"I am on medical leave," he says. "I have applied for early retirement."

"Wow, what a ride", I say reflecting on the past month of activities. I explain the new Jishuken network and the metrics that we have established now that Steve is no longer working for the competition.

Steve pulls out a gift box from his pocket and gives it to me. I open the box and see a Charles-Hubert watch.

"You notice that the new watch has a single time zone," he points out jovially. "You don't need a life-line anymore".

"Übung macht die meister," I say in my Neil impersonation voice.

"Übung schlägt die meister, Practice beats the Master" he says lifting his glass.

"Übung schlägt die meister", I say out loud.

-The tale of two supply chains: Toyota and GM-

Supply Chain Management

Part 2

Author's notes

-The tale of two supply chains: Toyota and GM-

Supply Chain Management

Chapter 19: An Interview with the Author

Recently a representative of the Supply Chain Institute sat down with the author at the Hilton Hotel, Chennai, to discuss the book and its contents.

Interviewer> First of all, why is this book presented as a study of contrasts?

Author> I firmly believe that Supply Chain is based on the edifice built on a set of guiding principles. Companies have a vision statement and a Supply Chain action plan that translates that vision into action, based on these guiding principles.

Toyota and General Motors have very different guiding principles. Therefore, this book uses their vision as bookends to describe the guiding principles, and in turn, the final finished product that we see as consumers.

Interviewer> In your view, what are the key differences between Toyota's Supply Chain philosophy and General Motors?

Author> Most Auto companies around the world have embraced lean TPS systems. They have moved away from old methods of mass manufacturing parts at the lowest cost per operation to lean manufacturing parts at their facility. However, at GM and some other companies, the supplier selection is still based on the lowest cost.

Many times, a lowest cost supplier may not be right supplier for a product. Think of this in terms of a contractor that you would hire for your house. Would you hire a contractor for your house strictly based on cost? Don't get me wrong. There may be situations where that lowest bidder may be the right contractor. But can you make the choice strictly on cost.

Overall, Toyota is driven the Toyota way and continuous improvement based on operational excellence. Throughout this book, I have contrasted the two approaches to supply chain. My point is, what you get in the end, is based on what you setup for expectations, along with choosing the right people and process to execute it.

Toyota way has a basic mantra on how people should be treated, and this includes suppliers. An outgrowth of this process is the Supplier relationship, that is demonstrated in metrics, such as the WRI.

Interviewer> How can the lessons learned in the Automotive Supply Chain help any business Supply Chain?

Author> Auto industry has made and continuous to make huge investments in supply chain around the world. These Supply Chain innovations have come in waves, led by trials in the auto industry (Shah, 2016). So many of the supply chain innovations driven by the industry are continuously market tested and are now available to every industry at large.

Going back to the industrial revolution, the Auto industry has traditionally been the driver for Supply Chain innovations. I can better explain this with a figure (See Figure 18.1). Ford, the champion of the automobile manufacturing, practically invented the world's first integrated Supply Chain. Circa 1910, Ford assets included a vertical integration of most of the components used in the Automobile. Ford Model T was very cost effective and propelled the young company into world leader status.

The next major change came with "the Toyota Way" in the 1970s and 1980s. Toyota worked with its tightly knit supply base, invented just-in-time delivery, and drove to leader status with an unbeatable quality. In the current day, China has risen to world status, by having a network of quality suppliers and a national level Supply Chain ecosystem.

The goal of Supply Chain is to provide a competitive weapon for the business model (Bowen, 2018). This is evident from Ford in 1910s, to Toyota in 1970s, to China today.

Now, looking into the future, with innovations such as 3D printing, cars could be made and assembled at the dealership. As an example, a 100% 3D printed Jeep vehicle is on display at the National Labs, Center for 3D printing, Knoxville, Tennessee. So, at this stage the entire Supply Chain will again become local or at the point of sale.

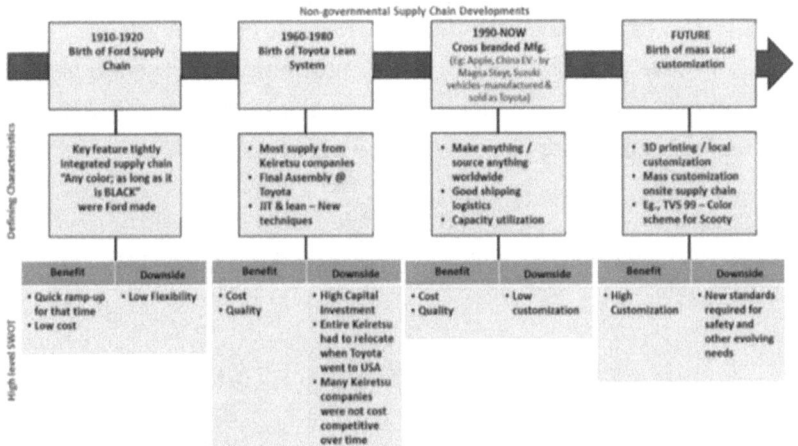

Figure 18.1: Supply Chain innovations – Led by Automotive Supply Chain

Interviewer> You are recommending a better supplier relationship. How do you go about creating a better relationship?

Author> Good question. Based on our research, we have created a synergy index for supplier relationship improvements. It is a specific rating scale to ensure that the supplier is the right fit for the company and the relationship is growing.

You can think of this almost like a marriage compatibility checklist that a premarital counsellor may give to young would-be couples.

Interviewer> What are the results that you have seen with such a supplier relationship improvement?

In a pilot study, we tracked a group of 8 suppliers for launching a new vehicle program. Here is a trend line chart (figure 18.2), that shows that our calculated synergy tracks well with the results in this synergy index.

The trend line shows the effectiveness of the theory of collective mutualism, that can be implemented across the globe, not only in Asia. The more synergy gives more returns, if the right suppliers are choosen for the ecosystem.

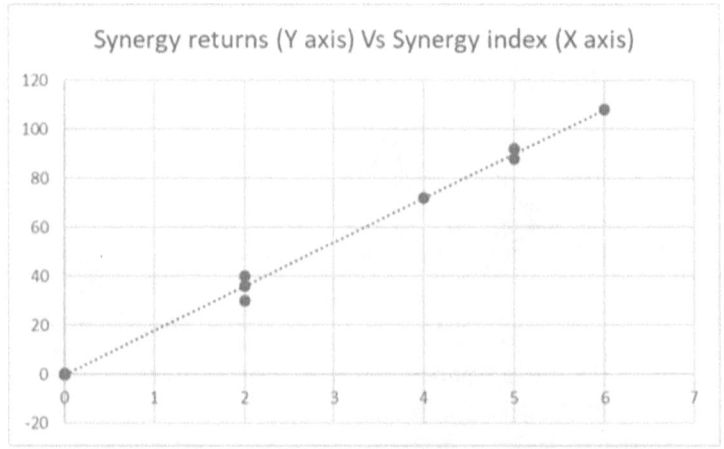

Figure 18.2: Returns from improved Supplier relationship,
The theory of Collective Mutualism

Interviewer> Before we get into Collective mutualism, let me ask, is there a hierarchy of value that a supplier brings to a relationship?

Author> In every relationship, each party brings a range of value to the relationship. It is important to put these value details into proper perspective. In a supplier business relationship, besides the auto companies themselves, suppliers have the prerequisite knowledge of the product's usage and how the suppliers' processing of the components adds value to the end customer.

Enclosed is a list of the common factors that are used to determine the value that the supplier brings into the relationship. Suppliers can be ranked based on their contribution to the business functions that include (and are not limited to) the following.

- Minimizing the total business risk: Business needs to manage the collective risk, between the supplier and the Automaker. The risk can be a global, systemic or local risk. For example, the global risk could be the effect of a pandemic.

- Minimize the total cost spent: The value of an Automobile is heavily dependent on the cost of its components. Automakers rank their suppliers based on the total spend with each supplier. If the ranked suppliers are considered as priority suppliers, then the Automaker may have a plan to manage these suppliers and their commodities to reach a minimum cost impact on the end-product. This is based on the premise that the suppliers that have a higher percentage of the total cost spent, may have a higher potential to improve the value.

- Improved supplier's capability & willingness to help the business: Supplier companies have their own agenda for growth and long-term profitability. Some companies are there to execute this business plan and may or may not be willing to invest in changes or continuous improvement. This focus by the supplier may not be in line with the Automaker's expectation.

- Alignment & congruence of goals: Identifying the common goals is the key ingredient in finding the right suppliers. This win-win philosophy can be managed to reach maximum potential for the partnership.
- Improved innovation: In a sea of suppliers, the suppliers that can innovate on new product features, new sourcing, new cost structures, etc., add value to the Supply Chain process.
- Stability of the supply base: Most suppliers in the Automotive Supply Chain across the world, undergo regular evaluation on their financial balance sheet before new business is awarded to them. Stability of the supplier is especially important.
- Project priorities and resource availability: Suppliers and Automakers should have the availability of the right capital and people to grow new Supply Chain relationship projects.
- Crucial to brand identity: Some suppliers may bring co-branding ability. When Mahindra & Mahindra Limited, an SUV and military vehicle manufacturer in India, was launching the new automated manual transmission, a new technology for India in 2015, the Mahindra Automotive Division worked closely with Ricardo plc, United Kingdom, which has an international track record

of automotive innovations. Marketing of this product in the Mahindra TUV jeep-style vehicle included the acknowledgement that Ricardo was the technical developer of this product[1].

- o Project wise investment versus return: Some projects will have an investment requirement and a cost benefit to the specific return expectation. Corporate internal rate of return in a range of expectation should be setup before undertaking this project.
- o Product and project complexity reduction: Asian automakers manage the complexity of the Supply Chain, so that there are minimal variations to the demand. Toyota production system is based on the Toyota Supply Chain principles (Iyer, 2004), that includes complexity reduction and managing variations.
- o Cross benchmarking and cross training: In Asia, most suppliers are required to train new suppliers, typically tier 2 or tier 3 suppliers, not directly supplying them. These mentee suppliers are not in the same field, with no long-term monetary benefit back to the mentoring supplier. For instance, a powertrain supplier will train underbody sub suppliers.

A value hierarchy can define the supplier contribution, in the following format, shown in figure 18.3.

---

[1] https://ricardo.com/news-and-media/news-and-press/ricardo-congratulates-mahindra-on-launch-of-india%E2%80%99

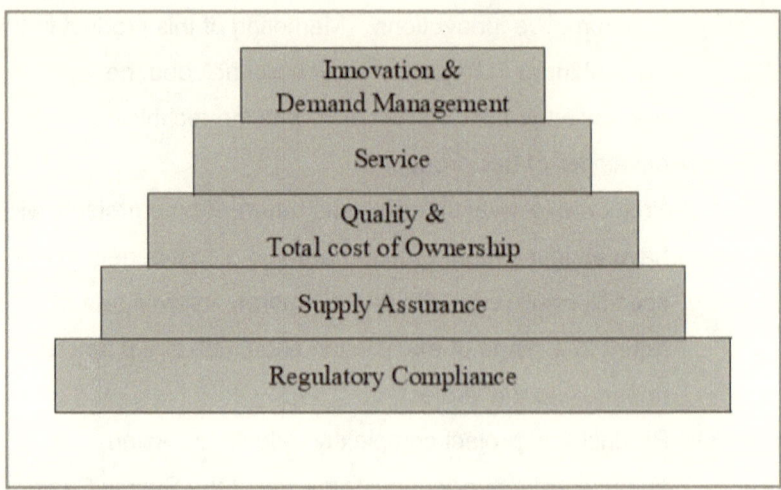

Figure 18.3: Example of supplier value hierarchy

Interviewer> How do you evaluate supplier maturity?

Author> The key ingredient of the Supply Chain is the ability of the supplier to create a lean Supply Chain for the high-volume products, but also create a parallel Supply Chain that is lean, and responsive, "the lean-agile" Supply Chain for the mid and low volume parts.

While the lean supply chain value stream handles about half the supply volume, the lean-agile stream handles the next step volume.

Table 18.1 shows the dimensions where Supply Chain maturity can be gaged.

Dimension/Critical Success Factor	Stage 0 (Reactionary)	Stage 1 (Transitory)	Stage 2 (Proactive)	Stage 3 (Dynamic)
Customer Service Management	Due care at each transaction. Ad hoc issues are handled at the operations meeting.	Equal treatment for all customers.	Herein a group of customers are identified as priority or strategic customers. These get special treatment, while the rest are treated alike.	The Supplier has gone the extra mile in segmenting customers and customer service plans. Each customer product can have its own segmented plan. Generally, Customers choose service level and pay.
Strategic business planning	Happens on an as needed basis.	Frequently and provides direction to supply chain. Typical functional scope is one year.	Supply chain has a limited cross functional scope.	The supplier has an integrated supply chain plan. Typical horizon is from 1 to 5 years.
Supply Chain and Operations (S&Op) coordination	Each day and each transaction focus. No long term clarity.	Budget based and monthly focus on planning.	Annual focus. Lead time reduction and long term issues are addressed.	Structured process with rolling periods, including long term capacity planning.
Workplace culture & Leadership	Adversial relationship between the employee and the management.	Limited engagement of the employees.	Consultation involvement of the workforce in decision making.	All decisions are done in high performance teams.
Subsupplier relationships	Transaction focus, limited data, no analysis capability	Competitive bid, price driven	Some strategic alliances established.	Strategic alignment of Supply & demand. Joint planning drives demand execution.
Information and IT Capabilities	Transaction focus, limited data, no analysis capability	Business data is available on fragmented pieces	Much improved Useful data but not universally available. Some drill down available	Real time actionable data for decision making
Demand forecast discipline	Demand is based on Gut feel.	Some forecasting, no ownership.	Some forecast is integrated in planning.	Single point data availability for all functional discussions.
KPI Management	Financial focus only	Some financial and some operational KPIs.	Cross functional balanced KPIs.	Balanced, cross functional scorecard, drives business.
Business improvement planning	Typically quick-fix 'stop bleeding' plans.	Cost reduction, no strategic focus	Structured appoach. Seeking breakthroughs	Continuous improvement toward goals. Kaizens implemented across functions and suppliers.
Innovation	Adhoc product development. Not clear on synergy.	R&D activities only. Less integration, identifies clear problem in	R&D or other department is fully involved. Not company wide	Formal cross functional innovation planning across the company
Organizational structure	Ad hoc changes and reporting structure	Some planned functional activities for organizational structure.	Some cross functional planning used to determine structure	Roles alignmed & responsibilities clearly marketed. Customer included in analysis
Electronic commerce	Limited. No strategy. Deployment is adhocvment.	In some parts of business,	Strategic planning and deployment based on cost/benefit.	Integrated and real time management. Cross functional processes are E enabled

Table 18.1: Expanded view of the Supply Chain Maturity Matrix (Adapted from various sources)

Interviewer> How is the hierarchy of supplier relationships different between Asia and the US?

Author> As I have said before, the supplier community has a wealth of competitive information and a strategic partnering can leverage this information for mutual benefit. Most supplier relationships may be rather transactional in nature, such as buying office supplies in an industrial company, where the purchased components do not add strategic value to the business.

But unlocking the supplier value, for some critical few suppliers can boost the innovation, operating efficiency and reduce the overall cost of the business.

In Asia, most supplier companies lie somewhere in the continuum from Arms -length supplier to a Group company. You can see this in figure 18.5.

The relationship is much higher down the scale in Asia, than in Europe and US. However, it is not necessary for an equity ownership relationship in supply base to develop good relationships.

Many new Automakers in Asia are leading the way in vertical integration, after outsourcing non-core functions. Unlocking the value may require a different level of interaction from treating at arms-length.

Many of the common transactions may require just a transactional relationship. In this relationship, order fulfillment is the main goal. Typically, no special care is necessary for the transaction, other than the purchase order issue and the payment terms for accounting. One step in the hierarchy above the transactional relationship, is the subcontractor relationship. In this case, the Automaker issues a statement of work (SOW) and the contractors bid on the job based on this SOW. The job is paid on completion or in stages based on the duration of the task and the trust ability between the supplier and the Automaker.

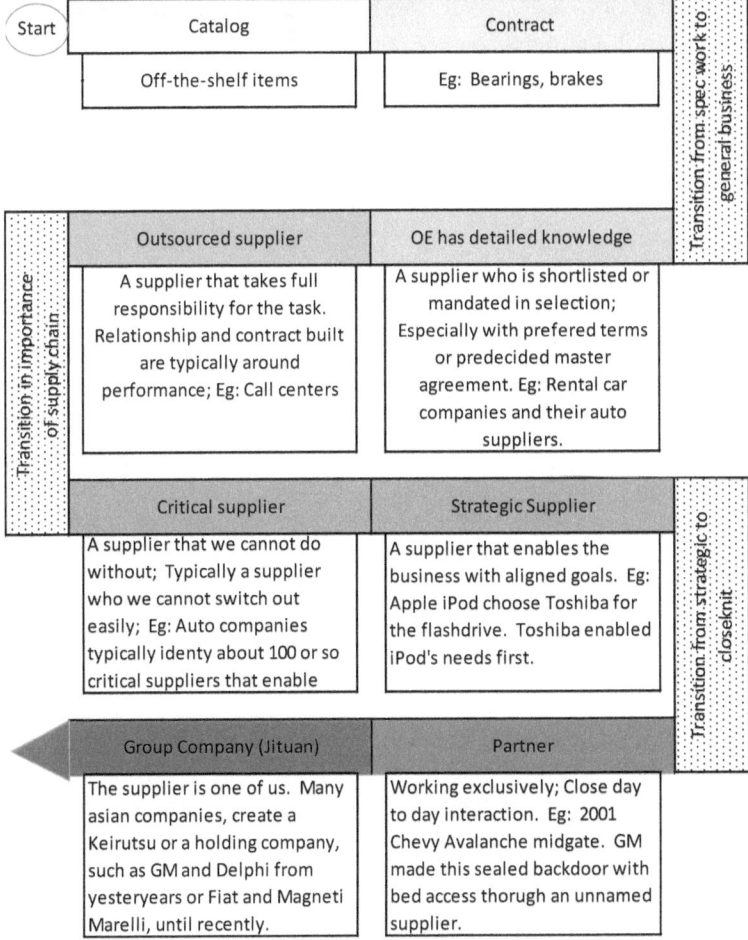

Figure 18.5: Common types of supplier relationships (Adapted from O'Brien, 2014)

The preferred supplier and the outsourced supplier are the next hierarchy level of supplier relationship.   In this the level of significance of the supplier is more crucial than the previous levels.   In unlocking the supplier benefits, we will focus on evaluating suppliers to see if they can be critical or strategic supplier at the third level of hierarchy or a partner at the fourth level. Finally, a supplier partner (such as LG Chem batteries for General Motors electric vehicles) and a group company status elevate to the highest level of supplier interaction.

Even if a group company status, such as purchasing a supplier company is not in the strategy, small changes in supplier relationship can have a big payback for both parties.

Interviewer> Contrast the Ecosystem model to Cost benefit model?
Author> Many Asian OE's follow the Toyota Supply Chain plan. Let's call this an Ecosystem+ model (Paul, 2019). In this model, automotive companies create an ecosystem of suppliers, with enhanced supplier relationships, such as being a preferred supplier or a member of the group company.

In the Ecosystem model (short for Ecosystem+), a supplier goes through a rigorous evaluation process to be selected for a new project. After the selection, the supplier has a higher chance of getting subsequent projects. Toyota has 90-95% return rate for its suppliers, while GM, Ford and FCA, typically have in the low 60s. This builds supplier loyalty and willingness to share operational problem solving details.

The relationship between the Automotive companies and their suppliers is more developed than the typical component pricing-based sourcing approach that is common in Automotive companies in US and Europe. It is also clear that the Asia centered suppliers with good connection to Automotive companies are continuing to substantially grow their business with subsequent business awards[2].

---

[2] https://hbr.org/2004/12/building-deep-supplier-relationships

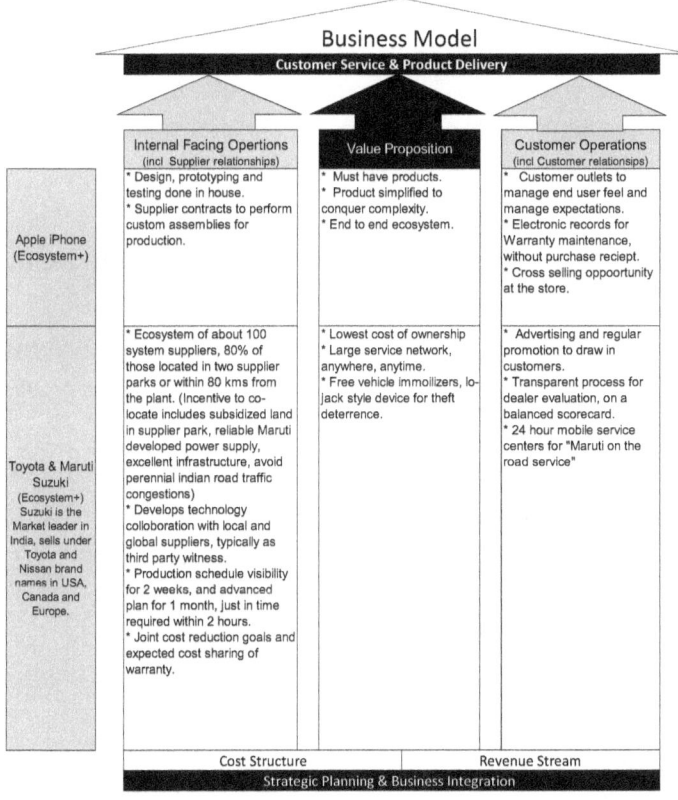

Figure 18.6: The Toyota and Apple Ecosystem+ model (Paul, 2019)

The Toyota and Apple iPhone versions of the Ecosystem+ model are shown in figure 18.6, using a three pillar business model (Paul, 2019). The left pillar documents the business strategies for the business internal operations and the right pillar documents the strategies for the external/customer operations. The middle pillar documents the value proposition that the business brings to the marketplace.

It should be very interesting that many of the Toyota suppliers have a similar business model to Toyota. One such supplier is

Maruti Suzuki, a subsidiary of Suzuki Motor Corporation, Japan. This entity makes small cars sold in the US and Europe under the Toyota brand name. We studied Maruti Suzuki in detail, due to the availability of quality information to understand Toyota's flow-down supply chain strategies.

Interviewer> How do you unlock the benefits of a better relationship?
Author> To unlock the benefits, let's start with a supplier relationship framework. This framework (figure 18.7) leverages the supplier relationship development as a key factor in growth and consists of 4 phases.

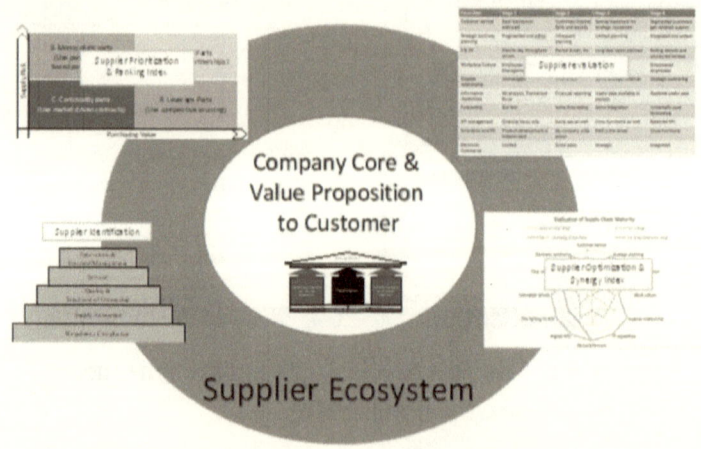

Figure 18.7: The Supplier Ecosystem framework

The supplier framework is the shaded circle with a white inner core, that represents the core of the company. Corporate business planning and the company's business model (shown earlier in figure 18.6) are the key parts for the inner core of this supplier framework.

The middle ring (gray shaded area) covers the supplier ecosystem. Suppliers transition from the environment (outside the gray circle) into the supplier ecosystem, through a four-phase process.

Let me explain the four phases of how to create the supplier ecosystem. You can think of it, just like the PDCA cycle. The PDCA cycle, or Plan-Do-Check-Act cycle is prevalent in Operations and Supply Chain Management problem solving today.

The four phases of the framework are
1. The Plan phase, using **the Supplier Identification process**
2. The Do phase, using **the Supplier Prioritization process**
3. The Check phase, using **the Supplier Evaluation process** and
4. The Act phase, using **the Supplier Optimization process.**

The Plan phase: The Supplier Identification process

In this phase, the suppliers are ranked based on the needs of the organization. In a typical automotive market, there may be over 7000 potential qualified suppliers worldwide. These suppliers can be classified into eight levels, as shown in Table 18.2.

The scoring system is shown in the table. It is based on the companies pre-established priorities and a well-defined hierarchy of values.

Supplier type	Supplier Identification scoring process

1. Arms-length - Transactional supplier 2. Sub-contractor 3. Preferred supplier 4. Outsourced supplier 5. Critical supplier 6. Strategic supplier 7. Partner 8. Group Company	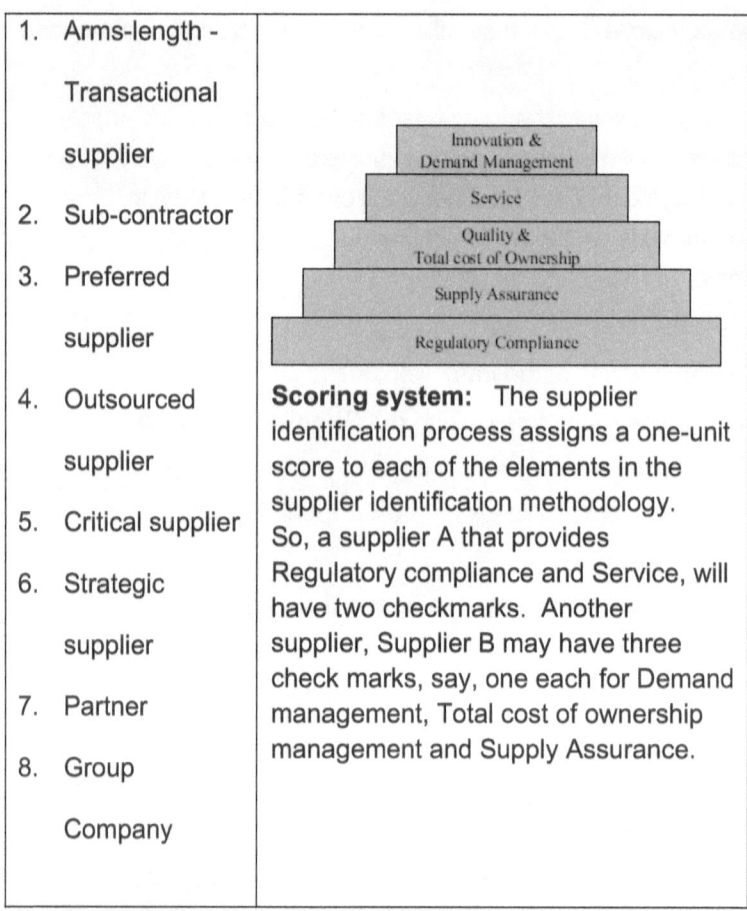 **Scoring system:** The supplier identification process assigns a one-unit score to each of the elements in the supplier identification methodology. So, a supplier A that provides Regulatory compliance and Service, will have two checkmarks. Another supplier, Supplier B may have three check marks, say, one each for Demand management, Total cost of ownership management and Supply Assurance.

Table 18.2: Scoring system for identifying the ranking index for the supplier

The Do Phase: The Supplier Prioritization process

The supplier prioritization process involves a ranking process and prioritization. A simple ranking process is to identify the importance of a particular commodity and to assign it to an appropriate supplier. The supplier would then be elevated or demoted to an arms-length supplier, subcontractor, partner etc. We choose a more intrusive approach for our processes, as shown in the ranking method (see table 18.2). For instance, supplier A with two units will be lower priority that supplier B with

3 or more units of scoring. The net result is a **ranking index** of all suppliers.

The Check & Act Phases: Supplier Evaluation and Optimization

Suppliers that are selected for this relationship growth process, should undergo quarterly progress evaluation to review the strategy and annual review to see if they are meeting the needs of supplier relationship goals. If the suppliers have not committed substantial improvements, they can be decoupled in the annual review stage. The supplier relationships are evaluated using the maturity rubric shown in figure 18.2. Suppliers can reach a mature relationship with optimal contribution and be mutually beneficial to the supplier and the Automaker. The annual review may upgrade or downgrade the ranking index based on the maturity progress of the supplier.

I will leave the detailed review of this supplier framework and the benefits of the method to more technical journals. My doctoral thesis includes the framework methodology as well.

Interviewer> How do you optimize the supplier relationship using synergy index?

Author> We used a series of surveys to identify a synergy index of the supplier, based on their technical capability, their management alignment and financial strength. For critical projects, suppliers that were high on the synergy index were chosen. You can see our results that I showed you earlier.

Interviewer> Give me some examples of the Jishuken network?

Author> In Japan, Toyota has the local supplier association which holds bimonthly general meetings, shares production details and reviews Jishuken learnings. In the US, the Bluegrass Automotive Manufacturing Association (BAMA) has a similar focus and effect in the supply base. The lessons learnt in improving quality, cost, culture and safety help members to develop and showcase best practices. Each supplier that benefits from Toyota Supplier Support will share their results in the network.

The MIT Sloan's research (Dyer, 2004) lists several supplier examples of benefits from such a network.

Interviewer> What is the background research for this book?

Author> During my expat work in Asia, I saw that unlocking the supplier value is done differently among Toyota suppliers than among other Automaker's suppliers. We started some early experimentation in Supply Chain to see if we can change the supplier relationship behavior and what its effects will be to the bottom line.

We collected information and surveys from 200 suppliers for this research. We then had in-depth interviews with supplier personnel from 36 Toyota in Asia and General Motors suppliers worldwide. These suppliers were evaluated for their Supply Chain strengths in China, India and the US. Ranking their Supply Chain maturity gave us clear direction for choosing new suppliers and executing successful supplier dependent new program launch.

Here is a sample set of results in figure 18.4. The supplier categories are:

- Logistics, docking and warehouse suppliers
- Toyota Tier 1 – Review of a specific supplier that was being evaluated
- Tier 2 – Supplier with no direct contracts with Automaker
- System integrators – Suppliers that provide entire systems; For example: Fuel systems for engines that includes fuel pumps, high pressure rails and low

pressure rails are provided by one company. These companies have the best synergy with the automaker.

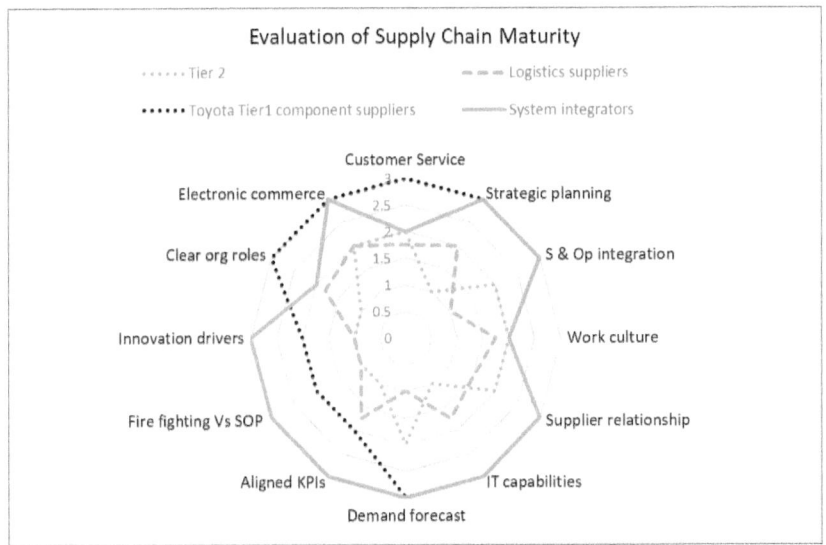

Figure 18.4: Supply Chain maturity measurement
(Source: Paul, 2019)

As you can see the Tier 1 system integrator, had the most developed supplier relationship management. This supplier was a system integrator with a conduit from the Automaker to the sub supplier, in passing the right build schedule to the sub suppliers, collecting the build components and delivering the integrated units to the Automakers assembly line.

In fact, the system integrators excelled in each metric compared to every other supplier category, except clear organizational roles. Logistics suppliers were the third most developed mature business model, while Tier 2 suppliers have substantial room to grow.

Interviewer> What is the Theory of Collective Mutualism?

Author> The Theory of Collective Mutualism states "What is good for the customer is good for the Supply Chain". Here, Toyota supply chain works as one entity, with Toyota as an equal partner to the suppliers within the supply continuum.

I believe that this is a measure of the loyalty of the suppliers to the Automaker and vice versa. Now many people may try to dismiss this as an Asia centric culture. However, Toyota has been able to reproduce the intent in the US as well. Our research shows that the supply base responds well to the improved relationship and mutual benefits.

Interviewer> In your doctorate thesis, you have compared the Theory of Collective Mutualism to the evolution theory of Endosymbiosis? How does it compare?

Author> The Asian supplier ecosystem behaves as a mutually beneficial organizational structure. This mutualism is not specific to one supplier and the Automaker, but to the Automaker and the supplier network, being collective in nature.

This Theory of Collective Mutualism is parallel to the theory of endosymbiosis, in evolutionary biology. In this theory, the mitochondria and chloroplasts are functioning organelles (almost full organisms), inside advanced life, ranging from amoeba to human beings. These organelles have specialized functions and are almost independent of the host life. Mitochondria are responsible for breaking down the energy for use in the human body and chloroplasts are elements that convert sunlight into energy.

The theory of endosymbiosis states that these organelles were most likely, fully functioning microbes during prehistoric times, that were ingested by the amoeba. By a stroke of nature, they lost their protein content (individual survival ability) and started functioning as organelles, part of the host, carrying out the specialized functions in modern life.

Interviewer> Granted that you have a good sample of supplier accounts. Can you get the account right with just the supplier accounts?

Author> In the first place, this book is not about the Toyota supplier accounts, but more based on the leverage through building a better supplier relationship. In addition to supplier accounts, our team was able to demonstrate the benefits by independently reproducing the gains in product cost and quality through improved supplier relationships.

Secondly, we started with a large sample size of about 200 suppliers. We, then narrowed the in depth discussion to 36 suppliers so that we can get a full detail description of their experiences. Statistically, this represents a 16.87% margin of error at 95% confidence level (or 13.67% margin of error at a 90% confidence level). However, since we were able to independently verify the results through the pilot study, we are at an extremely high confidence.

Thirdly, I believe that this book is unique, that it lays out our experiences. Toyota or any other Automaker is not going to let you see their operations in this much detail. So, I hope that I have been able to present this book as an insider look based on outsider accounts and an eye opener for those that may not be considering in investing in supplier relationship activities.

Interviewer> Very well, Dr. Paul. Best wishes and thank you for your time.

-The tale of two supply chains: Toyota and GM-

Supply Chain Management

Appendix

-The tale of two supply chains: Toyota and GM-

Supply Chain Management

Glossary & Abbreviations

- 8D Problem solving: A process of problem solving by identifying the root cause and closing out the key issues. This process was pioneered by Ford, and has 8 elements, hence 8D.
- A1 problem solving (pioneered by Toyota), where all the elements of problem solving are captured in one A1 size sheet. This is the tools for problem solving.
- CKD: Complete Knock down kit. The automotive industry's method of starting a new greenfield site. The startup process for launching a new plant typically includes a CKD kits of vehicle components, that are received at a new site. The vehicles are assembled from the CKD kits for a period of time, until after the regional Supply Chain and subassembly facilities are developed and are capable of the localization process.
- EDI: Electronic data interchange. This is a generic term covering many domains. Many suppliers have instituted electronic exchange of data for Engineering drawings (Enterprise CAD data), Purchase Order receipts and payment notification.
- FTR: First time right. This is a KPI (Key process indicator), in the Asian setting. The first time right metric insurers that the processes are properly debugged before start of serial production.
- Jituan: A Chinese conglomerate, typically a state-owned holding company. Each business in the Jituan has a

unique management but shares the common shareholders across business. Businesses in a conglomerate are obligated to support the sister companies, when making purchasing decisions.

- Keiretsu: A grouping of companies, found in Japan. Many companies have financial cross holdings in other companies, for instance in the Keiretsu under Toyota's control, all real estate transactions are managed through Towa Real Estate, Nippon Denso controls Electronics and Aisin is responsible for Auto Parts. Chaebol is the equivalent S. Korean conglomerate structure and is typically owned by a private family.
- KPI: Key Process Indicators. These are metrics for tracking business improvement.
- Maruti: Maruti Suzuki India Limited, the India Case study in this dissertation. This case study is interchangeably referred to as Suzuki or as Maruti.
- OEM: Original equipment manufacturers (Auto Companies in this dissertation context).
- Ranking Index: A priority list of suppliers to start the Supplier relationship synergy process. Ranking is defined in Chapter 6 and Chapter 9 with examples.
- SC or SCM: Supply Chain or Supply Chain Management.
- SCOR: The Supply Chain Operations Reference Model, developed by APICS.org. This is a popular framework in the US, since the reference data for benchmarking is available across industries.

- SGM: SAIC-GM Corporation, the China Case study in this dissertation.
- SRM: Supplier Relationship Management.
- Strategic Collaborative Management: This is the process of targeting high value suppliers for improving their strategic potential for collaboration.
- Supplier Improvement & Development: Supplier improvement is a process recommended by O'Brien (O'Brien, 2014), to systematically improve supplier performance through a 5 step process. This process is outside the scope of this dissertation.
- Supplier Performance Management: The evaluation, measurement and monitoring of the supplier performance and other practices to achieve supplier alignment to the KPIs. Such activities typically target cost reduction, risk management and continuous improvement as KPI metrics.
- SWOT analysis: Strength, Weakness, Opportunities and Threats Analysis, a popular analysis tool in strategic management.
- Synergy Index: The graphical plot of the financial appetite of the company, plotted against the management resolve. The top quadrant represents the best synergy index. The terms, Financial appetite and management resolve are defined in Chapter 10.
- TPS: Toyota Production System. Each company has a well-defined production system. TPS is the basis for most production principles at Asian supplier companies.
- VMI: Vendor Managed Inventory

- WIP strategy: A work in progress strategy. One of the common uses of a proper WIP strategy is the lead time reduction for agile Supply Chain. Parts made halfway and ready for further processing, can speed up production lead time. The other benefit is the **Optimal postponement option**, where a subcomponent is processed to the final step before the decision is made, whether it is going to be made into Product A or Product B. This is a common strategy in products such as iPhone, where the components are ready to be assembled into an iPhone 10 or iPhone X based on demand (Paul, 2019).

Recommended reading

1. Liker, J. (2004), *The Toyota Way, 14 Management principles from the world's greatest manufacturer,* McGraw Hill, NY
2. CIO Team (2009), Maruti Suzuki Gets New Markets with a Transparent Supply Chain, http://www.cio.in/case-study/maruti-suzuki-gets-new-markets-transparent-supply-chain, Downloaded 08 11 2018
3. Grajczyk, K. (2013), *Multi-tier Supply Chain Visibility in Automotive Industry, How do automotive OEMs gain transparency and visibility into their global Supply Chain?*, Lap Lambert Academic Publishing, Saarbrucken, Deutschland.
4. Paul, Shawn et all (2019), *The SMART Supply Chain*, Blue Rose publication, New Delhi, Delhi 110001, Publication July 2019.
5. O'Brien, Jonathan (2014), *Supplier Relationship Management: Unlocking the hidden value in your supply base*, Publisher: Koganpage.com, 2nd Floor, 45 Gee Street, London ECIV 3RS, United Kingdom.
6. Iyer, Ananth, et al (2009), *Toyota Supply Chain Management, A strategic approach to the principles of Toyota's renowned system*, Tata McGraw Hill Education Pvt Ltd, New Delhi.
7. Mentzer, John (2004), Fundamentals of Supply Chain Management: Twelve Drivers of Competitive

Advantage, Published: May 5, 2004, Sage Publications, Thousand Oaks, CA, USA

8. Emmett, S. et al (2016), The Relationship-Driven Supply Chain: Creating a Culture of Collaboration throughout the Chain, Routledge, New York, NY.

9. Manufacturing Group (2015), Honda, Toyota top supplier relationship index, Ford, GM, Nissan, FCA all decline in annual survey, https://www.todaysmotorvehicles.com/article/automotive-design-manufacturing-supplier-relationships-051915/, Published: May 19, 2015, Downloaded: Feb 1, 2020

10. Liker, Jeffrey & Choi, Thomas. (2004). Building Deep Supplier Relationships. Harvard Bus. Rev.. 82.

11. Nivisha Singh, Prashant Salwan, IIM, (2015), Contribution of Parent Company in Growth of its Subsidiary in Emerging Markets: Case Study of Maruti Suzuki, India Journal of Applied Business and Economics Vol. 17(1) 2015

12. Dyer, J. and Hatch, N., (2004). Using Supplier Networks to learn faster. MIT Sloan Management Review, 45(3).

13. Potter, A. and Wilhelm, M., (2020). Exploring supplier–supplier innovations within the Toyota supply network: A supply network perspective. Journal of Operations Management, 66(7-8), pp.797-819.

References

1. Ahrens, N. (2013), *China's competitiveness, Myth, reality and lessons for United States and Japan*, Center for Strategic and International Studies, 1800 K Street, NW, Washington, DC, page 3
2. Bhattacharya, S. Mukhopadhyay, D., Giri, S and Katra (2014), *Supply Chain Management in Indian Automotive Industry: Complexities Challenges and Way Ahead.* International Journal of Managing Value and Supply Chains (IJMVSC) Vol.5, No. 2, June 2014
3. Ecola, L., Rohr, C., Zmud, J., Kuhnimhof, T. and Phleps, P. (2014), *The Future of Driving in Developing Countries,* Institute for Mobility Research and Rand Corporation, Rand Corporation, USA, ISBN: 978-0-8330-8604-4
4. Shah, J. (2016), *Supply Chain Management, Text and Cases*, Pearson India Educational Services Pvt, Ltd, Chennai, India. ISBN: 978093-125-4820-6
5. Walter, E. & Walter, R. (2016), *Data Acquisition from HD Vehicles Using J1939 CAN Bus*, Society of Automotive Engineers, Detroit.
6. Stadtler, H & Kilger, C (2000), *Supply Chain Management and Advanced Planning, Concepts, Models, Software and Case Studies*, Springer-Verlag, Berlin, Heidelberg, New York.
7. Nakanishi, T. (2017), *India and the global auto industry's transformation, A technology shift is underway*, Asian Nikkei Review @

https://asia.nikkei.com/Business/China-India-and-the-global-auto-industry-s-transformation, Downloaded 06 11 2018.

8. Bowen, S (2018), *Total Value Optimization: Transforming your global Supply Chain into a competitive weapon,* Stephen J Bowen, SJDB LLC, PO Box 271, Duxbury, MA 02331
9. Cote, C (2015), Vehicle heat maps at https://insideevs.com/chevrolet-volt-heat-map
10. Sarkar, S. (2017), *Supply Chain revolution,* AMACOM, American Management Association, New York, NY 10019.
11. Liker, J. (2004), *The Toyota Way, 14 Management principles from the world's greatest manufacturer,* McGraw Hill, NY
12. Martin, J. (2007), *Lean Six Sigma for Supply Chain Management, A ten step process,* McGraw Hill, New York, NY
13. McBride, D. (2003), *The 7 Wastes in Manufacturing,* https://www.emsstrategies.com/dm090203article2.html, Downloaded 08 11 2018.
14. Durea, M and Strugariu, R. (2014), *An Introduction to Nonlinear Optimization Theory,* De Gruyter Open Ltd, Warsaw/Berlin.
15. Dollar, D. and Wei, S (2007), *Underutilized Capital,* Finance and Development, A quarterly magazine of the IMF, Website: users.nber.org/~wei/data/underutilized_capital.pdf, Downloaded 08 11 2018.

16. Price Water Coopers (2008), Sourcing and logistics in China, Cost processes and strategies of German companies in the Chinese market, Price Water Coopers and Bundesverband Materialwirtschaft, Einkauf und Logistik e. V (BME), Germany.
17. CIO Team (2009), Maruti Suzuki Gets New Markets with a Transparent Supply Chain, http://www.cio.in/case-study/maruti-suzuki-gets-new-markets-transparent-supply-chain, Downloaded 08 11 2018
18. Julka, T., Jain, SS & Singh, A. (2014), Supply Chain and Logistics Management Innovations at Maruti Suzuki India Limited, International Journal of Management and Social Sciences Research (IJMSSR), Volume 3, No. 3, March 2014
19. Grajczyk, K. (2013), *Multi-tier Supply Chain Visibility in Automotive Industry, How do automotive OEMs gain transparency and visibility into their global Supply Chain?*, Lap Lambert Academic Publishing, Saarbrucken, Deutschland.
20. Griffith, Erin (2017*), Why do startups fail, because hardware is hard,* https://www.wired.com/story/why-do-startups-fail-because-hardware-is-hard/, Wired Magazine, San Francisco, CA, USA, 9th September 2017.
21. Paul, Shawn et all (2019), *The SMART Supply Chain,* Blue Rose publication, New Delhi, Delhi 110001, Publication July 2019.
22. O'Brien, Jonathan (2014), *Supplier Relationship Management: Unlocking the hidden value in your supply*

base, Publisher: Koganpage.com, 2nd Floor, 45 Gee Street, London ECIV 3RS, United Kingdom.

23. Iyer, Ananth, et al (2009), *Toyota Supply Chain Management, A strategic approach to the principles of Toyota's renowned system*, Tata McGraw Hill Education Pvt Ltd, New Delhi.

24. Keller, Valerie (2015). A Business case for purpose, A Harvard Business Review Analytic Services Report, hbr.org/hbr-analytic-services, Downloaded: Nov 15, 2018.

25. Arena, U., Mastellone, M., & Perugini, F. (2003). Life cycle assessment of a plastic packaging recycling system. International I Journal of Life Cycle Assessment, 8, 92–98. https://link.springer.com/article/10.1007%2FBF02978432 . Downloaded: Jan 15, 2017

26. SJ Guest editorial (March 12, 2015), The Zara Gap – And Retail Denial, Sourcing Journal, https://sourcingjournal.com/topics/retail/zara-gap-retail-denial-thorbeck-25370/, downloaded 24 Nov 2018

27. Blokdyk, Gerardus (2019), SCOR Model - A Complete Guide - 2020 Edition, Published: September 6, 2019

28. Bolstorff, Peter et al (2012), Supply Chain Excellence: A Handbook for Dramatic Improvement Using the SCOR Model 3rd Edition, American Management Association, AMACOM, New York

29. Osterwalder, Alexander et al (2010), Business Model Generation: A Handbook for Visionaries, Game

Changers, and Challengers, John Wiley & Sons, New York, NY.
30. Mentzer, John (2004), Fundamentals of Supply Chain Management: Twelve Drivers of Competitive Advantage, Published: May 5, 2004, Sage Publications, Thousand Oaks, CA, USA
31. Emmett, S. et al (2016), The Relationship-Driven Supply Chain: Creating a Culture of Collaboration throughout the Chain, Routledge, New York, NY.
32. Manufacturing Group (2015), Honda, Toyota top supplier relationship index, Ford, GM, Nissan, FCA all decline in annual survey, https://www.todaysmotorvehicles.com/article/automotive-design-manufacturing-supplier-relationships-051915/, Published: May 19, 2015, Downloaded: Feb 1, 2020
33. Kelly, D., Rajan, R. and Goh, G., 2006. Managing Globalization. Hackensack, NJ: World Scientific Pub. 2006
34. Li-Wen Lin and Curtis J. Milhaupt, "We are the (national) champions: understanding the mechanisms of state capitalism in China", Published Date: Apr. 2013, Stanford Law Review, Stanford Law School (Vol. 65, Issue 4)
35. Freyssenet, M., 2009. The Second Automobile Revolution. Basingstoke: Publisher: Palgrave Macmillan.
36. Liker, Jeffrey & Choi, Thomas. (2004). Building Deep Supplier Relationships. Harvard Bus. Rev.. 82.
37. Nivisha Singh, Prashant Salwan, IIM, (2015), Contribution of Parent Company in Growth of its

Subsidiary in Emerging Markets: Case Study of Maruti Suzuki, India Journal of Applied Business and Economics Vol. 17(1) 2015
38. Dyer, J. and Hatch, N., (2004). Using Supplier Networks to learn faster. MIT Sloan Management Review, 45(3).
39. Potter, A. and Wilhelm, M., (2020). Exploring supplier–supplier innovations within the Toyota supply network: A supply network perspective. Journal of Operations Management, 66(7-8), pp.797-819.
40. Valentin, M., (2019). The Tesla Way. Amazon.com Services LLC.